Alison Leivesley is a solicitor, partner and head of the family department at Bindmans LLP. She is a Resolution Accredited Specialist in children law public, children law private, domestic abuse, forced marriage and 'honour' based violence. She acts for parents and carers in public law children proceedings with a specialism in cases with international elements and those involving forced marriage, so called 'honour' based violence and female genital mutilation. She is ranked as a star individual in Chambers and Partners Family/Children Law: Public Law Matters and ranked for Family/Children Law: Cross-Border Disputes. She is listed as a Leading Individual in the Legal 500. Alison was the winner of the Family Lawyer of the Year at the British Family Law Awards in 2024. She was Highly Commended at the Lexis Nexis 2023 Family Law Awards in the Partner of the Year category and was Female Trail Blazer of the Year at the 2024 Modern Law Awards.

A Practical Guide to Representing Parents in Care Proceedings

A Practical Guide to Representing Parents in Care Proceedings

Alison Leivesley

Law Brief Publishing

Published 2024 by Law Brief Publishing, an imprint of Law Brief Publishing Ltd
30 The Parks
Minehead
Somerset
TA24 8BT

www.lawbriefpublishing.com

Paperback: 978-1-916698-31-4

PREFACE

This book focuses on *some* of the topics relevant to practitioners when acting for parents and carers in issued applications for care orders. Some of the topics discussed are applicable at the pre proceedings stage.

The Public Law Outline was relaunched on 16 January 2023[1]. The President of the Family Division intends to reinvigorate the relaunch in October 2024[2]. There is a renewed focus on reducing delay and concluding care cases within the statutory 26-week time frame[3]. One of the Family Justice Board's six public law priorities for Local Family Justice Boards to achieve by 31 March 2025 is that at least 81% of all new cases are to be completed in 26 weeks.

Practitioners therefore need to identify, consider and progress the relevant issues in cases as early as possible.

The Institute for Crime and Justice Policy Research (ICPR), Birkbeck University and Revolving Doors are working in partnership on a research and policy project – "*Lived Experience of the Law*", funded by the Nuffield Foundation. In March 2024, their research "*Experiences of Public Law Care Proceedings: A briefing on interviews with parents and special guardians*"[4] was published. The experience of the participants was:

---

1 https://www.judiciary.uk/courts-and-tribunals/family-law-courts/re-launch-of-the-public-law-outline-plo/

2 A View from The President's Chambers: July 2024 - Courts and Tribunals Judiciary

3 Children Act 1989 section 31 (1)(a)

4 RD Experiences of Public Law Care Proceedings 24pp final.indd (nuffieldfoundation.org) Hunter, G, Thomas, M and Campbell, N

- They perceived themselves to be outsiders or bystanders at court proceedings, feeling "talked about".

- Most felt their lawyer did not adequately represent their lives or views or challenge aspects of evidence they considered to be wrong or unfair.

- They struggled to understand much of the legal terminology.

The aim of this book is to provide practitioners who are instructed by parents or carers in public law proceedings with a resource to assist them in presenting the best possible case and fully supporting their clients.

The law is correct as of 12 October 2024.

Alison Leivesley
October 2024

CONTENTS

CHAPTER ONE

THRESHOLD

Section 31 Children Act 1989

A court may only make a care or supervision order if it is satisfied:

> *(a) that the child concerned is suffering, or is likely to suffer, significant harm; and*
>
> *(b) that the harm, or likelihood of harm, is attributable to:*
>
> > *(i) the care given to the child, or likely to be given to him if the order were not made, not being what it would be reasonable to expect a parent to give him; or*
> >
> > *(ii) the child's being beyond parental control.*
>
> *(Children Act 1989 Section 31 (2))*

There are two elements to the threshold criteria:

(1) the existence of, or the likelihood of, 'significant harm', **and**

(2) the cause of that harm being attributable to either

(a) care given or likely to be given by a parent **or**

(b) a child is beyond parental control

Suffering, or is likely to suffer, significant harm

'Suffering' or is 'likely to suffer' must be in the present or the future. The past is not enough[1];

'Likely' means 'a real possibility' [2], 'a possibility that cannot be sensibly ignored having regard to the nature and gravity of the feared harm in the particular case[3];

'Harm' means ill-treatment or the impairment of health or development including, for example, impairment suffered from seeing or hearing the ill-treatment of another;

'Development' means physical, intellectual, emotional, social or behavioural development;

'Health' means physical or mental health;

'Ill-treatment' includes sexual abuse and forms of ill-treatment which are not physical.

(*Children Act 1989 section 31 (9)*)

'Significant harm' means harm that is "considerable, noteworthy or important"[4]. It is for the court to decide on the facts of a case whether harm is 'significant'.

---

1 *Re S & HS (Children)* [2018] EWCA 1282

2 *Re H (Minors) (Sexual Abuse: Standard of Proof) [1996] AC 563*

3 *Re B (Care proceedings: appeal) [*2013] 2 FLR 1075

4 *Humberside CC v B* [1993] 1 FLR 247

The 'harm' must 'be significant enough to justify the intervention of the State and disturb the autonomy of the parents to bring up their children by themselves in the way they choose'.[5]

Not all harm will be significant:

> "*Society must be willing to tolerate very diverse standards of parenting, including the eccentric, the barely adequate and the inconsistent. It follows too that children will inevitably have both very different experiences of parenting and very unequal consequences flowing from it...'; ... 'it is not the province of the State to spare children all the consequences of defective parenting. In any event, it simply could not be done". Re L (Care: Threshold Criteria)* [2007] 1 FLR 2050.

'Harm' can be cumulative to make it 'significant harm'.

Reliance may be placed on information acquired since the relevant date as to the state of affairs that existed at the relevant date *Re G (Care proceedings: Threshold Conditions)* [2001] 2 FLR 1111. Hale LJ considered the types of information that may have come to light since a case began:

- Information discovered after the relevant date that provides evidence of the facts at the relevant date e.g. medical evidence about the injuries that prompted removal, new complaints by the child about other forms of abuse within the home, admissions by parents. These can emerge during expert assessments the case.

- New events occurring during the proceedings which may or may not be capable of proving there was a risk of significant harm at the relevant time "*this raises more difficult questions because there*

[5] *Re MA (Care Threshold)* [2009] EWCA Civ 853

are obvious dangers of retrospectively validating a concern which was not in fact justified at the time".

- New events which introduce a completely different risk which did not exist at the relevant date.

Parental care

In assessing the standard of parental care, it is an objective test, and it includes acts as well as a failure to protect.[6]

The provision *"not being what it would be reasonable to expect a parent to give"* "*is not to be regarded as an abstract or hypothetical test but must be evaluated by reference to the circumstances the parent is confronting i.e. what would it be reasonable to expect of a parent in these particular circumstances, recognising that in a challenging situation many of us may behave in a way which might not objectively be viewed as reasonable. The test is not to be construed in a vacuum nor applied judgementally by reference to some gold standard of parenting which few (if any) could achieve. On the contrary, it contemplates a range of behaviour, incorporating inevitable human frailty. The reasonableness of the care given requires to be evaluated strictly by reference to the particular circumstances and the individual child*" Hayden, J *Lancashire County Council v M, F, W and Lancashire Clinical Commissioning Group* [2021] EWHC 2844 (Fam)

Beyond parental control

The fact of a child being beyond parental control is not capable on its own of satisfying the threshold criteria. Being beyond control must have caused significant harm or a risk of harm to the child.

There is limited case law when considering whether a child is beyond parental control as a threshold finding.

---

6 *Re A (Children) (Interim Care order)* [2001] 3 FCR 402

In *Re P (Permission to Withdraw Care Proceedings)* [2016] EWFC B2 HHJ Redgrave's view at first instance (disagreeing with *Re K* below) was that in care proceedings where the local authority was pleading the threshold criteria was met on the grounds of the child being beyond parental control, there needs to be an evidential connection with the parents' care.

In *Re K (Post Adoption Placement Breakdown)* [2012] EWHC 4148 (Fam) HHJ Bellamy sitting as a Deputy High Court Judge applied a Court of Appeal decision *Re L (a minor)* [1997] EWCA Civ 1268 and held that it is *not* necessary to prove parental fault to establish that a child is beyond parental control.

Re L considered the *Guidance to the Children Act Volume 1 para 3.25* "*… the second limb is that the child is beyond parental control …It provides for cases where, whatever the standard of care available, he is not benefitting from it because of lack of parental control. It is immaterial whether that is the fault of the parents or the child. Such behaviour frequently stems from distorted or stressed relationships between parent and child*".

This decision was approved in *T (A Child: Care Order: Beyond Parental Control: Deprivation of Liberty: Authority to Administer Medication)* [2017] EWFC B1. Recorder Howe QC stated "*in my judgment it is immaterial whether a child is beyond parental control due to illness, impairment or any other reason. The court simply has to consider if, on the facts, the child is beyond the control of the parent or carer. If that condition is satisfied the court then has to determine if the child is suffering from or likely to suffer significant harm as a result of being beyond the control of the parent. If the answer to that 2nd question is 'yes' then section 31 (2) (b) (ii) are satisfied*".

Current case law is clear that there does *not* need to be parental culpability for a finding that a child is beyond parental control.

These cases often involve teenagers and/or adoption breakdown. In these very difficult cases where there is a need for an order on welfare grounds, it is unhelpful for either the child to feel responsible for the breakdown of the family or blame to be apportioned to the parents.

Interim threshold

Section 38 Children Act 1989 sets out the threshold for the court to make an interim care order or an interim supervision order.

> *A court shall not make an interim care order or interim supervision order under this section unless it is satisfied that there are reasonable grounds for believing that the circumstances with respect to the child are as mentioned in section 31(2).*
>
> (*Section 38 (2) Children Act 1989*)

Interim threshold being met is not sufficient to permit interim removal of a child from parents. The court must find the child's safety demands immediate separation.

Relevant date

The 'relevant date' for determining whether a child '*is suffering*' significant harm is:

- at the time of the application for a care or supervision order; or
- at the time when the local authority initiated the procedure for the protection of the child concerned, provided those arrangements have been continuously in place until the time of the hearing.

Burden of proof

The burden of proof is on the local authority to establish the threshold criteria are met.

Standard of proof

The standard is the ordinary civil standard of the balance of probabilities. Described as a binary system, if a judge finds it more likely than not that something has taken place, it is treated as having occurred. If a judge does not find it more likely than not something occurred, it is treated as having not occurred.

The standard of proof is not affected by the seriousness of the allegation or the consequences.[7]

Threshold statement/ Threshold document

A 'threshold statement' is a written outline by the local authority of the facts which the local authority will seek to establish by evidence or concession to satisfy the threshold criteria. It should be limited to no more than 2 pages.[8]

Threshold documents should be compliant with the guidance in *Re A (A Child)* [2015] EWFC 11, essential reading for any care practitioner. The guidance in *Re A* was expressly approved by the Court of Appeal in *Re J (A Child)* [2015] EWCA Civ 222.

In *Re A,* Sir James Munby, the then President of the Family Division, reminded practitioners of 3 "*fundamentally important*" points:

(1) "*the elementary proposition that findings of fact must be based on evidence (including inferences that can properly be drawn from the evidence) and not on suspicion or speculation*" *(Re A (A Child)* (No 2) [2011] EWCA Civ 12, which carries two practical consequences:

---

7 *Re BR (Proof of Facts)* [2015] EWFC 41

8 Family Procedure Rules 2010, PD12A para 7.1

(a) local authority must adduce proper evidence to establish what they seek to prove. Hearsay evidence is, of course, admissible in family proceedings. But "*a local authority which is unwilling or unable to produce the witnesses who can speak of such matters first-hand, may find itself in great, or indeed insuperable, difficulties if a parent not merely puts the matter in issue but goes into the witness box to deny it.*"

(b) there needs to be a clear assertion. Schedules of findings sought often contain references to things that a parent "appears" to have done or that people have "reported" or "stated" or that there is "an allegation that…". This form of allegation "*is wrong and should never be used.*" The relevant allegation is not that someone 'appears' to have done something, it is that he 'did' it.

(2) link the facts relied upon by the local authority in its threshold with the conclusion that the child has suffered or is at risk of suffering a particular type of harm.

(3) "*society must be willing to tolerate very diverse standards of parenting, including the eccentric, the barely adequate and the inconsistent*" (*Re L (Care: Threshold Criteria)* [2007] 1 FLR 2050).

As Baroness Hale said in *Re B (A Child) (Care Proceedings: Threshold Criteria)* [2013] UKSC 33:

> "*We are all frail human beings, with our fair share of unattractive character traits, which sometimes manifest themselves in bad behaviours, which may be copied by our children. But the State does not and cannot take away the children of all the people who commit crimes, who abuse alcohol or drugs, who suffer from physical or mental illnesses or disabilities, or who espouse antisocial political or religious beliefs.*"

Practice points

- Look with a more critical eye at the allegations, particularly where the care plan is one for adoption.
- Are they clear in relation to the allegation itself?
- Is it clear what is alleged has caused significant harm?
- Is it specific about what significant harm has been suffered or is likely to suffer?
- Does it establish the causal link between the stated fact and the allegation of harm?
- Is there primary evidence, not suspicion or speculation?
- A concession from a parent should never obviate the need for a proven factual basis.[9]

9 *Re H (Parents with learning difficulties: risk of harm)* [2023] EWCA Civ 59

CHAPTER TWO

CRIMINAL INVESTIGATIONS / PROCEEDINGS

Police disclosure

From 1 March 2024 a revised protocol governing the disclosure of information between family and criminal jurisdictions has been in force. *The Disclosure of Information between Family and Criminal Agencies and Jurisdictions: 2024 Protocol* replaces the 2013 Protocol and Good Practice Model: *Disclosure of information in cases of alleged child abuse and care directions hearings*.

It covers all circumstances where there is to be an exchange of information and material between criminal and family agencies and jurisdictions. It relates to all private and public family law proceedings, including contemplated public law proceedings, and all material held by the police.

The protocol distinguishes between requests for information (in order to inform a request for material, or for an update about a case) and requests for material to be made using Annexes 1 and 5.

The protocol is in 3 parts plus annexes:

Part A: disclosure from the police to family proceedings

Part B: disclosure sought by an investigator

Part C: linked directions hearings

Annex 1: Application for disclosure for police information in family proceedings. The form to be used for applications for police material by local authorities and solicitors, other than by litigants in person.

Annex 2: Guidance notes for completing Annex 1 in private law proceedings.

Annex 3: Guidance notes for local authorities for completing Annex 1 in contemplated and ongoing public law proceedings.

Annex 4: A checklist for the judiciary when considering disclosure required from the police.

Annex 5: The standard order to be sought from the court for police material, for litigants in person and solicitors involved in private law proceedings.

Annex 6: The form to be used for applications made by the police for material.

The police should respond by providing disclosure as a general rule within 20 business days, unless an alternative timescale is approved by the court.

A request for information from a criminal court about a case, including information contained in materials kept by the court officer for the purposes of the case, may be made pursuant to *Criminal Procedure Rules Rule 5.*

Information about an investigation or, once charged, a prosecution may be sought in writing from the police or CPS respectively: the police should provide information about the investigation, the CPS about charge and prosecution (a "Part A Request for Information"). There is no prescribed form.

Linked directions hearings

In any case where the local authority, CPS or a judge in either the criminal court or family court considers it may be appropriate, a linked directions hearing in criminal and care proceedings can be listed. Early disclosure and listing of hearings are necessary in proceedings in a linked care and criminal case.[1]

Whenever the possibility of a linked directions hearing is raised in either criminal or family proceedings, the allocated criminal or family Judge shall, in the first instance, make enquiries of the other court through their Resident Judge or Designated Family Judge if that is necessary, in order to identify who is allocated to the case in the other court and when forthcoming hearings are.

Once identified, the allocated Family and Criminal Judges will liaise in order to enable the linked directions hearing to take place, remotely or otherwise.

The criminal case shall be listed before the judge at the Crown Court in public with the linked directions appointment in the care proceedings listed for hearing in private immediately afterwards. Subject to any specific objections raised by the parties, the advocates appearing in the criminal case may be invited to remain during the directions appointment in the care proceedings.

The local authority's legal representative and the CPS shall agree a schedule of issues identifying those matters which are likely to be considered at the linked directions hearing.

The directions hearing will be linked but not wholly combined because of the different parties and different procedural rules which apply. The judge shall determine whether it is appropriate for some or all of the

1 Family Procedure Rules 2010, Practice Direction 12A 5.8

directions to be issued at a joint hearing or separately and the order of any directions to be issued.

Example agenda items and matters to be considered at the linked directions hearing:

- Timetabling: the appropriate order of trials and ensuring expedition
- Disclosure: provision of material between the proceedings
- Expert evidence: identification, availability to provide opinion and attend court, experts' role in the criminal and care hearings
- Public interest immunity hearings
- Arrangements for the interviewing of children in care for the purpose of the criminal proceedings and any arrangements for the child to give evidence at any criminal or family hearing
- Transcripts: to ensure transcripts from earlier proceedings are available to subsequent ones
- Assessment or therapeutic input required by any child involved in the proceedings
- Reporting restrictions in both the criminal and the family court

<u>Disclosure sought by the police</u>

The Administration of Justice Act 1960, section 12 provides:

> *(1) The publication of information relating to proceedings before any court sitting in private shall not of itself be contempt of court except in the following cases, that is to say –*

(a) Where the proceedings –

i. Relate to the exercise of the inherent jurisdiction of the High Court with respect to minors;

ii. Are brought under the Children Act 1989 or the Adoption and Children Act 2002; or

iii. Otherwise relate wholly or mainly to the maintenance or upbringing of a minor.

The Family Procedure Rules 2010 (FPR 2010), r 12.73 provides:

(1) For the purposes of the law relating to contempt of court, information relating to proceedings held in private (whether or not contained in a document filed with the court) may be communicated:

(a) Where the communication is to:

.....

viii. A professional acting in the furtherance of the protection of children;

(b) Where the court gives permission; or

(c) Subject to any direction of the court, in accordance with rule 12.75 and Practice Direction 12G.

A local authority cannot automatically disclose to the police documents prepared specifically for the care proceedings or information (whether written or orally) which has emerged during the course of the proceedings once they have begun. The local authority can however disclose documents which were in existence prior to the proceedings beginning, even if they were then filed as evidence within the proceedings at a later date (for example child protection minutes and reports).

The police may seek information about family proceedings from a local authority in writing (a "Part B Request for Information") e.g. whether the local authority intends to obtain certain material, the date of a hearing or the dates of other procedural steps in family proceedings. There is no prescribed form. A Part B Request is outside the scope of Annex 6 under the Protocol. Information provided in response, may inform an Annex 6 request.

Family Procedure Rules Practice Direction 12G provides for a party in proceedings to provide the police and the CPS the text/summary of the whole or part of the judgment from family proceedings. A family judge can direct for their written judgment or agreed note prepared by the advocates to be sent to the police, for the purpose of criminal investigation or safeguarding or both.

Under *Administration of Justice Act 1960 section 12 (2)*, disclosure of court orders (the text or a summary of the whole or part of an order) does not require the permission of the Court, unless the court has expressly prohibited it.

Where a local authority is a party to proceedings, it must also provide a list (e.g. a copy of the redacted court index) of material within the family proceedings papers to the police, without describing the specific content. The local authority must where possible, and on the basis of the information provided by the police, highlight the documents on the index which are likely to be relevant to the criminal proceedings and for which an application for disclosure might be made.

If having received the judgment and/or list of material the police seek further information they must make an Annex 6 request and apply to the family court using by way of Form C2. If the material can be provided with the consent of the parties, a hearing may be unnecessary, and a consent order can be uploaded to the portal for the court's approval. The local authority (when they are party to proceedings) will assist in establishing whether the other parties consent to the provision of material.

It is unusual for the family court to disclose the whole bundle to the police. The Court should scrutinise the relevance to any criminal investigation of each of the documents sought by the police.

Re EC (Disclosure of Material) [1996] 2 FLR 725 sets out the test for applications for disclosure:

> *"In the light of the authorities, the following are among the matters which a judge will consider when deciding whether to order disclosure. It is impossible to place them in any order of importance, because the importance of each of the various factors will inevitably vary very much from case to case:*
>
> (1) *The welfare and interests of the child or children concerned in the care proceedings. If the child is likely to be adversely affected by the order in any serious way, this will be a very important factor.*
>
> (2) *The welfare and interests of other children generally.*
>
> (3) *The maintenance of confidentiality in children cases.*
>
> (4) *The importance of encouraging frankness in children's cases. All parties to this appeal agree that this is a very important factor and is likely to be of particular importance in a case to which s 98(2) applies. The underlying purpose of s 98 is to encourage people to tell the truth in cases concerning children, and the incentive is that any admission will not be admissible in evidence in a criminal trial. Consequently, it is important in this case. However, the added incentive of guaranteed confidentiality is not given by the words of the section and cannot be given.*
>
> (5) *The public interest in the administration of justice. Barriers should not be erected between one branch of the*

judicature and another because this may be inimical to the overall interests of justice.

(6) *The public interest in the prosecution of serious crime and the punishment of offenders, including the public interest in convicting those who have been guilty of violent or sexual offences against children. There is a strong public interest in making available material to the police which is relevant to a criminal trial. In many cases, this is likely to be a very important factor.*

(7) *The gravity of the alleged offence and the relevance of the evidence to it. If the evidence has little or no bearing on the investigation or the trial, this will militate against a disclosure order.*

(8) *The desirability of co-operation between various agencies concerned with the welfare of children, including the social services departments, the police service, medical practitioners, health visitors, schools, etc. This is particularly important in cases concerning children.*

(9) *In a case to which s 98(2) applies, the terms of the section itself, namely, that the witness was not excused from answering incriminating questions, and that any statement of admission would not be admissible against him in criminal proceedings. Fairness to the person who has incriminated himself and any others affected by the incriminating statement and any danger of oppression would also be relevant considerations.*

(10) *Any other material disclosure which has already taken place."*

Re EC has been confirmed as good law in *M (Children)* [2020] 1 FLR 50. In that case, position statements as well as statements of evidence were held to be disclosable to the police.

Re M also consider privilege against self-incrimination:

> *"Even where, in another case, the material that is subject to a disclosure application might contain potentially incriminating evidence, that factor would not establish a complete bar to disclosure. In such circumstances, the court would evaluate the application by giving careful consideration to the Re C factors before determining whether disclosure was necessary or proportionate".*

(*Re EC* is referred to in the authorities both as *Re EC* and sub nom as *Re C).*

Permission would also need to be given for disclosure of any material to the Crown Prosecution Service for use in any charging decision and ensuing criminal prosecution.

<u>Practice Points</u>

- What is the nature of the allegations in any ongoing police investigation?
- What information has already been shared with the police by the local authority?
- Is the request for material focused and proportionate? Or is it a "fishing expedition"?
- It is for the police to explain why *each* document is required.
- Have any of the documents been superseded? Are the police getting the most up to date information? Is the evidence skewed

by cherry picking documents that support a particular party's case?

- Medical records should be sought from the relevant NHS body/trust.

Police bail conditions

One of the issues that we as practitioners come up against in relation to interim contact is the impact of police bail conditions on a party's ability to spend time with a child.

Nottinghamshire County Council v The Mother and ors (police bail) [2024] EWHC 666 (Fam) was a High Court decision of Mrs Justice Lieven. Lieven, J urged the police to "*carefully consider*" the position and role of the Family Court when they come to determining bail conditions in the future. It was brought to the judge's attention that the police in that geographic area were routinely imposing bail conditions requiring no unsupervised contact with a child, in cases where there were family court proceedings, without including a caveat that there can be unsupervised contact if the family court, and/or the local authority agree.

Lieven, J found that the allocated family judge was in a "*much better position*" than the police were to determine any risks to the child in respect of contact, and whether unsupervised contact could be appropriately managed. In this case the allocated circuit judge had conducted a 5-day fact-finding hearing regarding serious injuries to a child, including having heard oral evidence and having had the children's guardian's welfare recommendations. Lieven J made the point that the police would neither have the detailed knowledge of the child's best interests in the case, nor the same expert advice as would the family trial judge.

CHAPTER THREE

EXPERT ASSESSMENTS

Who is an 'expert'?

'Expert' means a person who provides expert evidence for use in family proceedings.[1] Witnesses can usually only give evidence of fact, but expert witnesses are able to give opinion evidence in respect of their area of expertise.

Experts do not include social workers employed by the applicant local authority or children's guardians.[2] Rather, they are professional witnesses, with expertise in social work, who are expected to be able give their professional opinion on social work issues. They are not experts in other disciplines, so are expected to defer to the views of expert witnesses from other disciplines.

Treating medical professionals are usually witnesses of fact, but the court can permit a treating professional to give expert evidence under the *Children and Families Act 2014 section 13*. If that is allowed, the court must remain clear as to the difference between the role of the treating professional (who may, for example, need to have a continuing relationship with the parties) and that of the court appointed expert (this is considered further below).

In practice, an expert provides the court with specialist professional and technical knowledge not otherwise available from others in the case.

---

1 Family Procedure Rules PD25B 2.1.

2 Children and Families Act 2014 section 8

The court may control the evidence by giving directions as to[3]:

- the issues on which it requires evidence;
- the nature of the evidence which it requires to decide those issues; and
- the way in which the evidence is to be placed before the court;
- the court may use its power under this rule to exclude evidence that would otherwise be admissible;
- the court may permit a party to adduce evidence, or to seek to rely on a document, in respect of which that party has failed to comply with the requirements of this Part.

In the *President's Memorandum: Experts in the Family Court* [4] Sir Andrew McFarlane P set out principles applied by the Family Court when it considers whether to authorise or admit expert evidence.

The four criteria are:

- Assisting the court
- Does the expert have the necessary knowledge and expertise
- Impartiality

---

3 Family Procedure Rules 2010 Part 22 22.1

4 https://www.judiciary.uk/wp-content/uploads/2021/10/PFD-Memo-Experts.pdf

- Reliable body of knowledge or experience to underpin the expert's evidence[5]

The expert advises, and the judge decides on the basis of all the evidence.[6] It is thus open to the court to come to decision which is contrary to expert evidence. The court would need to give reasons for disagreement.[7]

No party may put expert evidence, in any form, before the court without the court's permission.[8] The court may refuse to admit evidence where permission of the court has not been obtained.

A court may only permit expert evidence to be adduced if it is of the opinion that the evidence is 'necessary to assist the court to resolve the proceedings justly'.[9]

The Court of Appeal in *Re H-L (Expert Evidence: Test For Permission)* [2013] EWCA Civ 655 held that the word 'necessary' should be construed as lying somewhere between "*indispensable*" on the one hand and "*useful*", or "*reasonable*", or "*desirable*", on the other hand, having the connation of the imperative, what is demanded rather than what is merely optional or reasonable or desirable'.

The general rule is that expert evidence will be given in a written report, and the court will not direct an expert to attend a hearing unless it is necessary to do so in the interests of justice.[10] It is now usual practice to permit experts to give evidence remotely.

---

5 *Kennedy v Cordia (Services) LLP (Scotland)* [2016] UKSC 6

6 *Re D (Care Order: Evidence)* [2010] EWCA Civ 1000

7 *Re MI (Care Proceedings)* [2013] EWHC 1073 (Fam)

8 Children and Families Act 2014, Section 13(5)

9 Children and Families Act 2014 section 13(6)

10 Family Procedure Rules 2010, r 25.9

Application for permission to instruct an expert

A party wishing to instruct an expert must apply for the court's permission as soon as possible and in public law proceeding, no later than the case management hearing (CMH).[11]

The application is made by:

- Form C2
- An application notice setting out:
  - The name of the proposed expert
  - The issues to which the expert evidence is to relate
  - Whether the expert evidence could be obtained from a single joint expert
  - The questions which the expert is to be required to answer[12]
  - Responsibility for instruction
  - Timescales
  - Experts' fees – hourly rates, hours needed to do the work
  - Any apportionment of costs

---

11 Family Procedure Rules 2010, PD 25C 4.1

12 Family Procedure Rules r 25.7(2), (3)

  - Whether there is any other evidence (whether obtained before or after the Start of proceedings)

  - Whether evidence could be given by another person on the matters on which the expert would give evidence e.g. social worker

- Copy of the experts CV

- Draft order[13]

- Court fee

When deciding whether to give permission to instruct an expert the court is to have regards to[14]:

- Any impact which giving permission would be likely to have on the welfare of the children concerned, including in the case of permission for a child to be medically or psychiatrically examined any impact which any examination or other assessment would be likely to have on the welfare of the child who would be examined or otherwise assessed,

- The issues to which the expert evidence would relate

- The questions which the court would require the expert to answer

- What other expert evidence is available (whether obtained before or after the start of proceeding

---

13 Family Procedure Rules r 25.7(2)(b)

14 Children and Families Act 2014 section 13(7)

- Whether evidence could be given by another person on the matters on which the expert would give evidence
- The impact which giving permission would be likely to have on the timetable for, and duration and conduct of, the proceedings
- The cost of the expert evidence,
- Any matters prescribed by Family Procedure Rules.

Identifying an expert

National Standards for Expert Witnesses have been inserted into *Family Procedure Rules 2010, PD25B* requiring an expert to comply with certain standards:

- *Area of competence is appropriate to the issue(s) upon which the court has identified that an opinion is required, and relevant experience is evidenced in their CV.*
- *Been active in the area of work or practice, (as a practitioner or an academic who is subject to peer appraisal), has sufficient experience of the issues relevant to the instant case, and is familiar with the breadth of current practice or opinion.*
- *Working knowledge of the social, developmental, cultural norms and accepted legal principles applicable to the case presented at initial enquiry, and has the cultural competence skills to deal with the circumstances of the case.*
- *Expert is up-to-date with Continuing Professional Development appropriate to their discipline and expertise, and is in continued engagement with accepted supervisory mechanisms.*

- *If the expert's current professional practice is regulated by a UK statutory body they are in possession of a current licence to practise or equivalent.*

- *If the expert's area of professional practice is not subject to statutory registration (e.g. child psychotherapy, systemic family therapy, mediation, and experts in exclusively academic appointments) the expert should demonstrate appropriate qualifications and/ or registration with a relevant professional body on a case by case basis. Registering bodies usually provide a code of conduct and professional standards and should be accredited by the Professional Standards Authority for Health and Social Care. If the expertise is academic in nature (e.g. regarding evidence of cultural influences) then no statutory registration is required (even if this includes direct contact or interviews with individuals) but consideration should be given to appropriate professional accountability.*

- *The expert is compliant with any necessary safeguarding requirements, information security expectations, and carries professional indemnity insurance.*

- *The expert has undertaken appropriate training, updating or quality assurance activity – including actively seeking feedback from cases in which they have provided evidence-relevant to the role of expert in the family courts in England and Wales within the last year.*

- *The expert has a working knowledge of, and complies with, the requirements of Practice Directions relevant to providing reports for and giving evidence to the family courts in England and Wales. This includes compliance with the requirement to identify where their opinion on the instant case lies in relation to other accepted mainstream views and the overall spectrum of opinion in the UK.*

Preliminary enquiries can be made of experts under *Family Procedure Rules 2021 PD25C 3.2.* the expert can be provided with:

> (a) *the nature of the proceedings and the issues likely to require determination by the court;*
>
> *(b) the issues in the proceedings to which the expert evidence is to relate;*
>
> *(c) the questions about which the expert is to be asked to give an opinion (including any ethnic, cultural, religious or linguistic contexts)*
>
> *(d) the date when the court is to be asked to give permission for the instruction (or if – unusually – permission has already been given, the date and details of that permission);*
>
> *(e) whether permission is to be asked of the court for the instruction of another expert in the same or any related field (that is, to give an opinion on the same or related questions);*
>
> *(f) the volume of reading which will need to be undertaken;*
>
> *(g) whether or not permission has been applied for or given for the expert to examine the child;*
>
> *(h) whether or not it will be necessary for the expert to conduct interviews – and, if so, with whom;*
>
> *(i) the likely timetable of legal and social work steps;*
>
> *(j) any dates in the Timetable for the Child which would be relevant to the proposed timetable for the assessment;*
>
> *(k) when the expert's report is likely to be required;*

(l) any hearing dates at which the expert may be required to give evidence (in particular the Final Hearing); and whether it may be possible for the expert to give evidence by telephone conference or video link

(m) the possibility of making, through their instructing solicitors, representations to the court about being named or otherwise identified in any public judgment given by the court;

(n) how the instruction will be funded and if legally aided, the applicable legal aid rates

The Law Society have produced pro forma documents to assist in instructing experts, including templates for preliminary enquiries of an expert, letters of instruction, and specimen questions.[15]

Guidelines on the instruction of experts who are based overseas have been issued by the Family Justice Council and endorsed by the President of the Family Division.[16]

Instructing an expert the same sex as your client

Re: A (A Child: Appeal: Case Management Decision: Identity of Expert) [2024] EWHC 1669 (Fam) was an appeal in a private law case, made on several grounds including whether the appellant's objection to being assessed by a male psychologist was adequately considered. Ms Justice Henke found that the judge at first instance was wrong to order a male psychologist to carry out a global psychological assessment of the family when the mother had stated she would feel traumatised during and following an assessment by a male psychologist after suffering rape and other forms of male violence including past abuse by a male medical

15 https://www.lawsociety.org.uk/topics/family-and-children/instructing-experts-in-family-and-children-court-proceedings

16 *Experts Committee of the Family Justice Council Guidelines* [2012] 1 FLR 889

professional. The High Court found that the mother as a result of her past abuse would not be able to give her best evidence during the assessment process contrary to *Part 3A* and *PD3AA Family Procedure Rules 2010* (see also Chapter 4).

Difference between treating doctor and expert

A treating doctor is not automatically precluded from giving expert evidence to the court, and it *may* be appropriate in some cases. It is important to distinguish between an expert who is a treating doctor and an expert who is reporting. Care must be given to ensure that the role of the treating doctor does not become blurred.

In Re F (A Child: Fact-Finding Appeal) [2019] EWCA Civ 1244 a community paediatrician who saw a child at hospital and wrote a child protection medical report subsequently became involved in a experts' meeting. She was then effectively giving expert evidence and was granted permission to give "expert evidence for use in proceedings"[17] despite her assertion that she was not *able* to act as an expert witness.

Therapeutic relationships and patient confidentiality should not be undermined. That can tip the balance away from seeking 'expert evidence' from treating doctors and other health professionals.

Moylan LJ noted in *Re F* the important difference between treating professionals and expert witnesses. A treating professional will "*self-evidently have a very different focus to an expert witness*". For instance, doctors treating adults who have a patient focused approach may not be used to the child centred approach of the court.

[17] Children and Families Act section 13(6) and (7))

Treating clinicians who are called as witnesses are subject to the same duties to the court as an instructed expert and should be sent a letter of instruction.[18]

Practice points

- Consider what expertise you need for your case. Best practice is for the earliest possibly identification of any issue that will need expert evidence and instructing the right experts as quickly as possible.

- Request and scrutinise an up-to-date CV.

- Consider the competence of the expert to undertake the specific requirements of your case. Are they currently in practice in their area of expertise and fully up to date with current standards of practice? Or do they only do court expert work?

- Does the expert meet *each* of the National Standards for Expert Witnesses.

- Do not rely on expert witness commissioning companies as a potential marker of good quality reports.

- Has the expert ever served on a public or professional body, committee or panel? Was any report or decision to which the expert was a party published?

- Is the expert undertaking all work required for the assessment? Is there evidence of others conducting parts of the assessment? If so, have you seen their CVs, are they suitably qualified?

---

18 *Oldham MBC v GW and PW* [2007] EWHC 136 (Fam)

- Ask for confirmation of how many family court reports the expert has undertaken in the last 12 months.

- Research any reported/published judgments the expert has been named in for any criticism or positive feedback.

- Check for any complaints to their regulatory body (if regulated by a UK statutory body).

- What is the impact on the court timetable of instructing the expert?

Letters of Instruction

Where a direction has been made for the instruction of a single joint expert, the instructions are to be contained in a jointly agreed letter unless the court directs otherwise.[19]

The party responsible for instructing the expert shall prepare (in agreement with the other parties where appropriate) a letter of instruction to the expert.[20]

The requirements for the letter of instruction are contained in *Family Procedure Rules PD25C, para 4.1.*

The Annex to *PD25C* sets out suggested questions that may be asked of a child mental health professional, paediatrician, and of an adult psychiatrist or applied psychologist.

The Law Society's sample questions for experts cover a wide range of disciplines:

---

19 Family Procedure Rules 2010, r 25.12(1)

20 Family Procedure Rules 2010, PD25C, para 4.1

- clinical psychologists
- forensic psychologists
- child psychologists
- psychiatrists
- child and adolescent psychiatrists
- adult psychiatrists
- radiologists
- ophthalmologist
- independent social workers
- paediatricians
- GPs

https://www.lawsociety.org.uk/topics/family-and-children/instructing-experts-in-family-and-children-court-proceedings

However, specific questions for individual families should be considered.

Questions for parenting assessments should be based on the Department of Health framework[21].

Practitioners should consider simplified wording for questions to make sure that reports are accessible for parents.

---

21 https://basw.co.uk/sites/default/files/resources/basw_123020-9_0.pdf

An appropriate expert instructed should be asked to make recommendations about how a vulnerable parent can participate effectively in proceedings. Any specific needs a parent has or where there are concerns that a parent has specific needs should be highlighted in the letter of instruction.

Consideration should be given as to whether an appointment between the expert and the parent should take place remotely given the limitations of remote assessments. For example, the impact on the parent and assessor establishing a rapport, the opportunity for a parent to mask any difficulties, parents' access to technology and their digital literacy, not knowing who else is on the link. The British Psychological Society and Association of Clinical Psychologists have provided guidance on remote psychological assessments (produced during COVID-19) setting out that there are clear limitations and additional considerations when psychologists conduct assessments remotely[22].

Where the letter of instruction is not agreed, the court may determine the instructions on the written request of any party.[23]

Unless the court directs otherwise, the instructing parties are jointly and severally liable for the payment of the expert's fees and expenses.[24] (See paragraph funding experts below)

Where the court has delivered a judgment, particularly a fact-finding judgment, that will be the starting point for future decision making and

---

22 https://cms.bps.org.uk/sites/default/files/2022-06/Expert%20witnesses%20undertaking%20remote%20psychological%20assessments.pdf ; https://acpuk.org.uk/wp-content/uploads/2020/05/Expert-witness-guidance-during-Covid-19-mw.pdf

23 Family Procedure Rules 2010 r 25.12(2)

24 Family Procedure Rules 2010 r 25.12(6)

any account of the background should take the judgment as its primary source. It is likely to create a confusing or misleading picture otherwise.[25]

An expert should be asked at the earliest stage whether another expert is required to bring a skill or expertise not already involved.[26]

Expert's report

An expert has 'an overriding duty to the court that takes precedence over any obligation to the person from whom the expert takes instructions or by whom the expert is paid'.[27]

The duties of an expert are set out in *Family Procedure Rules 2010, Part 25,* supplemented by *PD25B*. The contents of the expert's report are prescribed by *PD25B, para 9.1.*

A party wishing to clarify an expert's evidence can ask written questions. Any party may put written questions about an expert's report, whether the expert is a single joint expert or instructed by another party.[28]

Unless the court directs otherwise, the questions:

- must be proportionate;
- may be put once only;
- must be put within 10 days beginning with the date on which the report was served;

25 *The London Borough of Newham v the mother & others* [2023] EWFC 60

26 *Oldham MBC v GW and PW* [2007] EWHC 136 (Fam)

27 Family Procedure Rules 2010, PD25B, para 3.1

28 Family Procedure Rules 2010, r 25.10(1)

- must be for the purpose only of clarification of the existing report (and not to raise fresh issues);
- must be copied and sent to the other parties.

Family Procedure Rules 2010, r 25.10(1)

A second expert opinion should be considered where expert medical evidence has become 'pivotal' and is difficult to challenge in the absence of further expert report e.g. medical imaging.[29]

Within 10 working days after the final hearing, the party responsible for instructing the expert must inform the expert in writing of the outcome of the hearing and the use made of the expert's evidence, and must provide the expert, within 10 business days of that party receiving it, with the order and any transcript of the court's decision.[30]

Experts' meetings

All too often the terms experts meeting and professionals meeting are used interchangeably as if they mean the same thing.

The court may direct that an experts' meeting should take place following receipt of the experts' reports.[31]

The structure and content of the experts meeting are set out in the *Family Procedure Rules*[32] and the relevant practice directions – unlike professionals' meetings, which are not provided for in the Rules but are a recognised forum for discussion and gathering information. In *Re L*

---

29 *W v Oldham Metropolitan Borough Council* [20025] EWCA Civ 1247

30 Family Procedure Rules 2010, r 25.19

31 Family Procedure Rules 2010, PD25A, para 6.2

32 Family Procedure Rules 2010 r25.16

(Care: Assessment: Fair Trial) [2002] EWHC 1379 (Fam), Munby J gave guidance:

> *"Where it is proposed that the social workers and/or guardian should meet with a jointly appointed or other sole expert witness instructed in the case (what I will refer to as a 'professionals' meeting', as opposed to a meeting of experts chaired by one of the legal representatives in the case – usually the children's guardian's solicitor);*
>
> > *(a) there should be a written agenda circulated in advance to all concerned;*
> >
> > *(b) clear written notice of the meeting should be given in advance to the parents and/or their legal representative, accompanied by copies of the agenda and of all documents to be given or shown to the expert and notice of all issues relating to or criticisms of a parent, or a non-attending party, which it is intended to raise with the expert;*
> >
> > *(c) the parent, or non-attending party, should have a clear opportunity to make representations to the expert prior to and/or at the meeting on the documents, issues and/or criticisms of which he or she has been given notice;*
> >
> > *(d) a parent or other party who wishes to should have the right to attend and/or be represented at the professionals' meeting;*
> >
> > *(e) clear, accurate, full and balanced minutes of the professionals' meeting (identifying in particular what information has been given to the expert and by whom) should be taken by someone nominated for that task before the meeting begins;*

> *(f) as soon as possible after the professionals' meeting the minutes should be agreed by those present as being an accurate record of the meeting and then be immediately disclosed to all parties."*

In preparing for an experts meeting, the lead solicitor should circulate to the other parties a draft agenda of questions to be put to the experts. The agenda and/or list of questions should be sent to the experts not less than 2 clear business days before the meeting. *Practice Direction PD25E* sets out a clear timetable for submitting questions to the experts. Questions received on the day of or during the meeting should not be accepted.

Where the court has directed the preparation of a Statement of Agreement and Disagreement all the experts should sign that. It should be filed and served no later than 5 days after the meeting has taken place.[33]

Psychologists

The instruction of psychologists in family law proceedings has been the subject of debate within family law and has been picked up by the mainstream media.[34]

Some professions have a protected title, which may only be used by those who are validly registered. Other professions are not protected. The generic term "psychologist" is not protected and may be used by any individual whether they are registered or not. "Clinical psychologist" "forensic psychologist", "counselling psychologist", "educational psychologists" and a few others are protected titles which may only be used by those who are validly registered.

---

33 Family Procedure Rules 2010, r 25.16(3); PD25E, para 3.1(e)

34 https://www.independent.co.uk/news/uk/crime/parliament-mps-wales-england-royal-courts-of-justice-b2289170.html

In *Re C (Parental Alienation; Instruction of Expert)* [2023] EWHC 345, a mother appealed seeking a re-hearing of her private law children case after her children were removed from her care. She claimed the jointly instructed expert who assessed her family was neither regulated nor appropriately qualified as a psychologist. The appeal was not successful, but the President of the Family Division addressed the wider issue of psychologists as experts. He highlighted how the "*open-house nature of the term psychologist is unhelpful and potentially confusing*". He stopped short of saying the family courts should never appoint those who are "*unregulated*" and it was a matter for the psychological profession, and ultimately parliament, whether a "*tighter regime should be imposed*". However, "*A lesson plainly to be drawn from the present case is the need for clarity as to an expert's qualification and/or experience.*" Registration with the Health and Care Professions Council (HCPC) or charted status with the British Psychological Society provides a "*reliable one-stop method of authentication*".

In every case where the instruction of a psychologist is considered the court should identify whether the proposed expert is HCPC (The Health and Care Professionals Council) registered. A sensible practice, where the expert is un-registered, is for the court to indicate in a short judgment why it is appropriate to instruct them.[35]

Following *Re C* the Family Justice Council and the British Psychological Society jointly published updated Guidance on the use of Psychologists as Expert Witnesses in the Family Court in England and Wales: https://www.bps.org.uk/guideline/psychologists-expert-witnesses-family-courts-england-wales.

It is a very useful read for all practitioners in care proceedings setting out:

35 *Re C ('Parental Alienation': Instruction of Expert)* [2023] EWHC 345 (Fam)

- The types of issues psychologists can assist with, including but not limited to psychological impact of trauma and/or abuse; neuro-developmental conditions (e.g. Autism Spectrum Disorder (ASD) / Autism Spectrum Condition (ASC)); attachment styles and interpersonal relationships.
- Explanation of regulation.
- Protected titles and regulation of practitioner psychologists.
- Detailed description of each type of practitioner psychologist including areas of work, proficiencies and exclusions at registration and typical training.
- Examples of case instructions and suggested hours to undertake assessment.
- Checklist for instructing solicitors.
- Checklist of necessary minimum information for a psychologist expert's CV including HCPC registration number (if applicable), HCPC specialist protected title (if applicable).

Regulation by HCPC can be checked on the HCPC register. Ensuring registration is a fundamental issue.

Drug and alcohol testing

If there is expert interpretation of the results of drug and alcohol testing, it will be 'expert' evidence.[36]

---

36 *Richmond London Borough Council v B, W, B and CB* [2010] EWHC 2903 (Fam)

There are a variety of tests which can be used for testing for drug and alcohol usage. Each type of sample testing has its own limitations. Testing forms part of the overall evidential picture. Hair strand drug test results should not be used to reach evidential conclusions in isolation from the other evidence (results indicating low levels of use, in particular, should be treated with caution).[37]

A court will not authorise the instruction of a toxicology expert who is not certified as meeting the international standards set out in *Family Procedure Rules 2010, PD25G.*

Options for drug testing

- Head hair testing – can provide an overview or segmented month-by-month analysis of up to 12 months, or longer if the length of the hair allows. A segmented analysis can show trends such as an increase or decrease in use. It is not always possible to segment head hair samples, e.g. if the hair is very curly.

- Arm and body hair testing – can provide an overview analysis for twelve months Different sites show a different time period e.g. chest around four to nine months, arm around two to six months. A body/arm hair sample is less susceptible to passive contamination.

- Fingernail samples – can give an approximate overview of the previous 6 months. Due to the way nails grow and the available nail that can be collected, the analysis can only give an overview. Fingernails can give a more complete picture if scalp hair is damaged. As fingernails grow, drugs and their metabolites pass from the blood vessels below the nail into the keratin fibres where they are trapped. As nails are thicker than hair strands more

37 *Re H (A Child) Proceedings: Hair Strand Testing) [2017] EWFC 64*

of a substance can be captured. Nails are less affected by external influences compared to hair.

- Toenail samples – can cover an approximate overview 12 – 18 months

- Oral fluid testing – saliva is useful for detecting recent drug use and allows for non-invasive specimen collection via a mouth swab. It detects recent drug use after ingestion up to 2 days, although this can depend on the substance taken. Results can be offered instantly or sent off to the laboratory.

- Urine testing – The window of detection for urine is 36 hours. Drugs including cocaine, methamphetamine and MDMA can be present in urine for roughly 3–5 days, but cannabis can stay in urine for as long as 28 days after chronic use.

In the context of hair strand and nail testing, some testing laboratories have a cut-off threshold they apply to test results to simplify reporting and interpretation of test results. Cut-offs are used to divide results into two categories – 'positive' and 'negative' or sometimes 'positive' and 'not detected'. Terms to describe levels detected e.g. high, medium and low are based on the cut off level and the testing laboratory's individual database of results. That means that different laboratories will define high, medium and low in accordance with their own data, not absolute and shared definitions.

A positive result means metabolites of drugs have been found in the sample, rather than drugs have been used. A negative or not detected result means that the drug is either at a lower level than the cut off or it was not in the sample, rather than drugs have not been used.

There are many factors that can affect the presence and level of drugs e.g. hair dyes, straightening and surprisingly hair colour. Using cut off levels does not take these in account. Cut off levels cannot be used in isolation.

The recent case of *Re D (Children: Interim Care Order: Hair Strand Testing)* [2024] EWCA Civ 498 has brought into focus again the evidential value of hair strand drug testing along with its reliability and its limitations. In that case the judge at first instance authorised the local authority to remove 3 children, all of whom were the subjects of interim care orders in its favour, from the care of their maternal grandmother and maternal uncle, with whom they were living. That decision was largely based upon 3 sets of hair strand drug testing reports. On appeal, permission to appeal the decision to remove was granted along with permission to adduce fresh evidence. The case highlighted the need for investigation and careful consideration of hair strand test results.

Mr Justice Cobb stated that in all cases involving drug testing evidence it is vital that the advocates:

- Draw the judge's attention to what the science can and cannot tell you, as explained *Islington v M*[38] and *Re H*[39];

- Carefully examine the hair strand test reports in full; as far as it is thought helpful or appropriate to do so, they should distil their contents accurately so as to provide the Judge with a reliable summary, not just a rehearsal or précis of the general 'Summary' or 'Opinion' section;

- Assist the Judge to consider the hair strand test results in the context of the whole of the evidence, including:

    (a) Statements of those who are alleged to have exposed the children to the drugs identified;

---

38 *London Borough of Islington v M and another* [2017] EWHC 364 (Fam)

39 *Re H (A Child) Proceedings: Hair Strand Testing)[2017] EWFC 64*

(b) Other evidence (i.e., from observation) which may suggest drug use within the home;

(c) Other evidence which may suggest that drugs are not used within the home;

(d) The presentation of the children and the adults;

(e) The history of the family generally.

(f) Observations of children and adults, history of family generally

> *"This is all the more important, of course, in cases where the test results are in the lower range*".

<u>Options for alcohol testing</u>

Using blood tests only or hair tests only cannot provide the information required for clear interpretation. For alcohol the following are recommended:

- Hair strand testing for EtG and FAAEE – can provide an overview analysis for up to 6 months for chronic excessive alcohol consumption. Tests should be undertaken for alcohol bio markers EtG (Ethyl Glucoromide) and FAAEE (Fatty Acid Ethyl Esters) sometimes referred to as fatty acid ethyl ester, ethyl palmitate (EtPa).

  In order to provide the court with the best information, tests should be undertaken for both because of the differences in the markers, the different ways in which they are incorporated into hair and their different susceptibilities. as approved by Moylan, J in *Richmond London Borough Council.*

As also set out in the judgment of Moylan, J *in Richmond London Borough Council* there are limitations in hair strand testing for alcohol:

(a) the level of EtG or FAEEs found in a hair sample reflects the average consumption of alcohol over the whole of the period covered by the sample. It does not determine the manner in which such alcohol might have been consumed: i.e. number of times used, amount consumed, the amount consumed on each occasion

(b) hair tests should be used only as part of the evidential picture for the judge to evaluate [40]

(c) because of the respective strengths and weaknesses of each of the tests for EtG and FAEEs both tests should be used

(d) results produced by the tests should be used only for the purposes of determining whether they are or are not consistent with excessive alcohol consumption. They cannot be used to distinguish between social drinking and total abstinence

(e) similarly, the tests are not designed to establish abstinence or social drinking

(f) research shows 10% of the results will be false positives and 10% will be false negatives

(g) any evidence based on the testing of 1cm segments of hair is unlikely to be sufficient to support conclusions as to the level of alcohol consumption

---

40 *London Borough of Islington v M and another* [2017] EWHC 364 (Fam), *Re H (A Child: Hair Strand Testing)* [2017] EWFC 64

(h) the fact that either EtG and/or FAEEs are found to be present in hair in measurable quantities does not mean (i.e. does not support the proposition) that the subject of the test has consumed alcohol. Either could be found to be present as a result of other factors including through alimentary alcohol (e.g. from some breads) and endogenous alcohol (through normal human metabolism)

(i) FAEEs are not easily washed out of hair but can be affected by hair treatments – bleaching will reduce their concentration while the use of products containing alcohol will increase their concentration.

(j) FAEEs can be detected in hair as a result of exposure to alcohol in the atmosphere (such as a pub if there is a large amount of alcohol vapour in the air)

(k) the extent to which EtG is incorporated in hair will depend on a number of factors including how people sweat and the length of a person's hair; in addition, there are significant biological variations between people

(l) EtG is susceptible to being washed out and, on the other, being capable of being incorporated as a result of the use of products on the hair which contain alcohol

- Blood testing for LFT,CDT, GGT – CDTr, MCV and Peth – the alcohol biomarkers carbohydrate deficient transferrin (CDT) and phosphatidylethanol (PEth) are commonly tested for and can provide a window of detection of up to four weeks prior to the test.

  CDT is less influenced by other factors in comparison to other blood tests although it can be elevated for other reasons e.g. pregnancy. It is possible not to have an elevated CDT level and be drinking excessive levels of alcohol. A negative CDT result cannot be used to definitively show an individual has not consumed excessive levels of alcohol.

PEth is not affected by medication or health problems and provides a detection period of up to four weeks prior to sample collection.

Some laboratories also test for GGT – CDTr, a combined index based on y-glutamyltransferase (GGT) and carbohydrate deficient transferrin (CDT) and MCV mean corpuscular volume.

A liver function test (LFT) now referred to by medical professionals as liver blood tests[41] can give a snapshot of potential liver damage due to excessive alcohol use. However, it can give a 'false positive' if the damage is unrelated to alcohol usage e.g. liver damage due to medical conditions or with use of certain medications. The liver can repair itself and in some cases markers can return to normal once someone stops consuming alcohol.

Unlike hair, blood tests cannot be influenced by external or environmental factors or adulterated. But as blood markers can be affected by other influences, using several blood tests reduces, but does not eliminate, those issues.

- Urine testing for EtG – the window for detection is over a period of approximately 72 hours. The results can be affected by how someone metabolises alcohol, medical conditions, medications.

- Fingernail testing for EtG – can give an approximate overview of the previous 6 months. EtG alcohol markers are trapped in the fingernail as it grows.

41 https://britishlivertrust.org.uk/information-and-support/living-with-a-liver-condition/liver-blood-tests/

- Toenail samples – can cover approximate overview of 12 – 18 months.

- Breathalyser testing – provides instant results but is of limited use in proceedings as it only shows alcohol consumption for the few hours before the testing. Results can be affected by products like mouthwash. Results can be affected by how someone metabolises alcohol, and/or exercise.

- Transdermal Alcohol Continuous Testing – is an alcohol testing bracelet that allows for 24-hour testing. The bracelet provides information on alcohol excreted through the skin every 30 minutes. Every 30 days of the testing period, a report can be prepared detailing the alcohol consumption events or any attempts to tamper or obstruct the bracelet. Complete abstinence cannot be confirmed but very low alcohol consumption can be determined. Good for monitoring current and future alcohol intake and can be used as part of a treatment programme encouraging abstinence.

  The costs of testing may be claimed on a client's legal aid certificate if this has been ordered by the court and the testing does not form part of therapy or a support programme.[42]

Reports

Experts need to:

> "*fully and faithfully*" explain their finding. "*The expert must (a) describe the process, (b) record the results, and (c) explain*

[42] *Legal Aid Agency Guidance on the Remuneration of Expert Witnesses in Family Cases para 5.17* Guidance on the Remuneration of Expert Witnessesv7.docx (publishing.service.gov.uk)

> *their possible significance, all in a way that can be clearly understood by those likely to rely on the information*"

and

> "*The writer [of a hair strand test report] must make sure as far as possible that the true significance of the data is explained in a way that reduces the risk of it becoming lost in translation. The reader must take care to understand what is being read, and not jump to a conclusion about drug or alcohol use without understanding the significance of the data and its place in the overall evidence.*" *Re H (A Child: Hair Strand Testing)* [2017] EWFC 64.

<u>Practice Points</u>

- Instruct test providers in the same way as any other expert, following the Practice Direction including sending a letter of instruction, if interpretation of the results is needed.
- Consider whether it is necessary to instruct an independent expert to undertake a full forensic investigation to interpret any results. Toxicologists are the only people who should be interpreting results.
- Read deeper into the data within each report looking at the more complex, nuanced picture as well reading the summaries.
- Minimum required detection levels differ, depending on the drug being tested.
- Different testing companies have different guidance on cut off points. It would be good practice to use the same company to undertake all of the testing.

- Check with your client they have prepared for the sample collection by providing as much context for the testing company as possible including having a list of medication taken, medical conditions suffered from, pregnancy, products used on their hair, type of hair and a full history of their substance use e.g. what they used, when they last used, how frequently, etc.

- Prepare your client for the processes involved in taking a sample, including the type of sample that will be taken.

- Always test for EtG and FAAEE in hair strand testing for alcohol with a cross check by using PEth testing.

- Obtain a direction for a range of tests (hair, blood, urine) especially if it is important to show abstinence.

- Ensure you obtain directions for regular testing.

- To avoid difficulties with payment by the Legal Aid Agency, ensure the court direction sets out the length of time the testing should cover; the exact type of testing being undertaken e.g. specific the type of blood tests to be done (the type of analysis required e.g. is it an overview/standard testing basis or on a month-by-month/segmented testing basis; specifies the types of drugs that should be tested.[43]

- Look for other evidence of abstinence/low usage.

---

[43] *Legal Aid Agency Guidance on the Renumeration of Expert Witness para 5.15;* Legal Aid Agency Electronic Handbook 10.14: Drug and Alcohol Testing

- Consider the need for a psychiatric assessment undertaken by an addiction specialist who can review the test results and look at the overall evidential picture.

DNA testing

F (Children) (DNA Evidence) [2007] EWHC 3235 (Fam) Anthony Hayden QC, sitting as a deputy High Court judge, gave guidance on the instruction of experts to carry out DNA testing and the content and format of their report:

> "*32.*
>
> "(i) *Any Order for DNA testing made by the Family Courts should be made pursuant to the Family Law Act 1969.*
>
> *(ii) The Order should specify that it is being made pursuant to the Act and either the company who is to undertake the testing should be named or the Order should direct that the company identified to undertake the testing is selected in accordance with the Act, from the Ministry of Justice Accredited List. Only accredited companies may be instructed.*
>
> *(iii) The taking of samples from children should only be undertaken pursuant to the express order of the court. If a need arises for further samples to be taken, that should be arranged only with the approval of the court. If all the parties agree on the need for further samples to be taken, the application may be made in writing to the Judge who has conduct of the matter. These requirements should be communicated to the identified DNA company in the letter of instruction.*
>
> *(iv) Save in cases where the issue is solely confined to paternity testing, where the identified company may have its own standardised application form, all requests for DNA testing should be by letter of instruction.*

(v) The letter of instruction should emphasise that the responsibilities on DNA experts are identical to those of any expert reporting in a family case and that their overriding obligation is to the court. Further, if any test carried out in pursuance of their instruction casts any doubt on or appears relevant to the hypothesis set by their instructions, they should regard themselves as being under a duty to draw that to the attention of the court and the parties.

(vi) Any letter of instruction to a DNA company should set out in clear terms precisely what relationships are to be analysed and, where the information is available, the belief of the parties as to the extent of their relatedness. (In recent decades British society has become much more culturally diverse. Some cultures have different attitudes to consanguine relationships, others include children within the family for a variety of reasons (usually highly laudable) who may have remote or indeed no genetic connection to the adults. In these cases, separate statements from the parties setting out the family history and dynamics is likely to be helpful).

(vii) The letter of instruction should always make clear that if there appears to the DNA expert to be any lack of clarity or ambiguity in their written instructions, or if they require further guidance, they should revert to the solicitor instructing them. The solicitor should keep a note or memorandum of any such request.

(viii) The reports prepared for the court by the DNA experts should bear in mind that they are addressing lay people. The report should strive to interpret their analysis in clear language. Whilst it will usually be necessary to recite the tests undertaken and the likely ratios derived from them, care should be given to explain those results within the context of their identified conclusions.

(ix) Particular care should be taken in the use of phrases such as "this result provides good evidence". That is a relative term (and was here overtaken by stronger contrary evidence). Such expressions should always be set within the parameters of current DNA knowledge and should identify in plain terms the limitations as to the reliability of any test carried out. A "likelihood ratio" by definition is a concept which has uncertainty inherent within it. The extent of uncertainty will vary from test to test and the author of the report must identify and explain those parameters (e.g. It is not always possible to demonstrate half sibling relationship by DNA testing, even where it is given that a biological relationship exists".

(x) In this case, Orchid Cellmark conducted all the tests undertaken by Anglia DNA but also some further additional tests. Though it is not a feature of the evidence here, I would also add that where any particular test and subsequent ratio of likelihood is regarded as in any way controversial within the mainstream of DNA expertise, the use of the test and the reasons for its use should be signalled to the court within the report."

Practice Points

- Instruct a testing company on the Ministry of Justice accredited list: https://www.gov.uk/get-a-dna-test/if-youre-getting-a-test-to-use-in-court.

- Instruct test providers in the same way as any other expert, following the Practice Direction including sending a letter of instruction.

- Any letter of instruction to a DNA company should set out in clear terms precisely what relationships are to be analysed and, where the information is available, the belief of the parties as to the extent of their relatedness.

- Consider whether separate statements setting out family history are necessary.

- To ensure payment from the Legal Aid Agency the direction should set out how many tests and of whom are being undertaken, how many collection fees are being incurred and a whether a report is being drafted[44]. The Legal Aid Agency have separate rates for testing the sample and preparation of the report and guidance on collection fee.

- If you have an adult client who does not have capacity to consent to provide a DNA sample, an application should be made to the Court of Protection for a "best interests" decision about taking a sample. Declarations as to the protected party's (P's) best interests and orders facilitating the taking of bodily samples for non-therapeutic purposes fall within the scope of *Mental Capacity Act 2005 sections 15 and 16.*[45]

Parenting assessments

Parenting assessments are directed by the court to look at a parent/carer's skills in looking after a child, their knowledge about what a child needs and their ability to meet those needs until they reach adulthood.

The court is not looking for the "perfect parent". "S*ociety must be willing to tolerate very diverse standards of parenting, including the eccentric, the barely adequate and the inconsistent" Re L (Care: Threshold Criteria)* [2007] 1 FLR. The court are looking for "good enough" parenting, a

44 *Legal Aid Agency Guidance on Remuneration of Expert Witnesses para 5.18 – 5.22*

45 *Bagguley v E* [2019] EWCOP 49 (25 October 2019)

concept derived from the work of British psychoanalyst Donald Winnicot.[46]

4 key elements of good enough parenting:

- meeting children's health and developmental needs
- putting children's needs first
- providing routine and consistent care
- acknowledging problems and engaging with support services

The assessment of capacity to change adds a time dimension and asks whether parents, over a period of time and if provided with the right support recognise the need for change, are ready, willing and able to make the necessary changes to ensure their child's wellbeing and safety, engage with the process and sustain those changes over time.

Types of parenting assessment

Although parenting assessments will include standardised assessment tools, consideration of which type of assessment and the specific support available is best for your client is important. (See also Chapter 4 parents with additional needs)

- Local authority in house parenting assessments
    - If the assessment is undertaken by the allocated social worker, it is a professional the parent already has a working relationship with

46 *The Child, the Family, and the Outside World* (Penguin 1973), D.W Winnicot

  - Perceived lack of independence from the local authority felt by parents, whether that is an assessment undertaken by the allocated social worker or another in house local authority resources.

  - Is the local authority able to provide specialist assessments e.g. parents with additional needs?

- Residential parenting assessments.

  - An assessment which can balance risk whilst keeping families together.

  - Can consider whether there are significant gaps in knowledge/evidence about parental functioning, or relationship dynamics.

  - Has the potential to provide evidence of whether parents have the capability to provide 'good enough' parenting, on a consistent basis, within a relatively short timeframe, showing strengths and areas for improvement.

  - Scope for training and advice for parents and for therapeutic input.

  - Provision of support around substance misuse, mental ill-health or domestic abuse.

  - It is an artificial environment and is not day to day life in families own homes and communities.

  - High levels of surveillance and the intensity of the process can be difficult for parents particularly if they have led an independent life.

  - Families are often placed a distance from home. This can be an advantage providing distance from negative influences. Or it can be detrimental as it removes parents from their community and support networks.

  - Local support and relationships are not tested in a family's own community meaning that risks can re-emerge/remain when families return to their own home.

  - The level of support on return home will not be the same as during the assessment.

- Community-based parenting assessment

  - An artificial environment if taking place in a family centre.

  - Limited time spent observing parents.

- Independent Social Workers (ISWs)

  - An option where there is/or is a perception of lack of independence or a prejudged outcome if the local authority assesses, e.g. in high conflict cases.

  - ISWs can be chosen with specific expertise e.g. teenagers, risk of exploitation, or specific cultures.

  - This option can allow sufficient time to fully assess complex cases and cases where has not been a positive working relationship between parents and the allocated social worker or local authority.

  - Many ISWs have substantial experience in child protection work and many have previously held senior positions in local authorities or have been children's guardians prior to ISW work.

- As an ISW they are 'experts' subject to the Family Procedure Rules 2010 part 25.

- There are few evaluations of advantages and disadvantages of ISWs.[47]

- Parent and child/baby foster placement.

  - Provides 24-hour support to manage risks.

  - Traditionally placements have been for mothers and babies.

  - These assessments can be difficult for parents to cope with, as they are in a stranger's home, being observed.

  - Including fathers/partners may present a difficult dynamic for foster carers to manage.

  - Many local authorities, particularly in the London Boroughs, have difficulties recruiting new foster carers particularly those willing to offer parent and child placements.

- Multi-disciplinary family assessment by ISWs, Psychologists and Family Support Workers, as well as Psychiatrist and Forensic Risk Experts if required

47 The Contribution of Experts in Care Proceedings: Evaluation of Independent Social Work Reports in Care Proceedings', Brophy, J; Owen, C; Sidaway, J; Jhutti-Johal, J; 2012

  - The team work together to assess the family unit and parenting capacity, in their own home or in a community.

- Reverse residential assessment/ supported community assessment (24/7 in the home/)

  - Delivered within the family home and in the local community.

  - It offers an opportunity for parents to demonstrate their parenting and access their own support network and local resources.

  - It is familiar and natural family environment in the family home.

  - Package of support, guidance and monitoring on a 24-hour basis

  - Avoids placement moves.

  - Avoids the dynamics and distractions that there can be with a residential assessment and living with other families.

  - Can tailor the support needed.

- Specialist assessment for parents (please also see Chapter 4 parents with additional needs)

  - ParentAssess or CUBAS approach is based on the Department of Health Assessment of Children in Need and their Families but uses a range of tools to help parents with additional needs engage with and understand the assessment process.

- Strengths based framework with assessors able to identify what might help a parent with specific needs.

- Suitable for all parents including those with additional needs.

- Assessors have to be ParentAssess or CUBAS trained to use the assessment tools.

- Simple traffic light system to help parents express their views and assessors give feedback on a parent's progress. Red significant concern; amber some concerns, monitoring needed; green no concerns. Colour-coded ratings of risk and support needs are included in the assessment report.

- A shorter simplified visual report is provided for parents. "Things that are good and you do well, things I'm concerned about, what I am going to tell the court".[48]

- The assessment uses photos of things in everyday life, rather than cartoons or drawings.

Funding parenting assessments

It is long established that residential assessments (or viability assessments used to assess whether residential assessments should go ahead) are to be paid for by the local authority.[49]

The Legal Aid Agency *Guidance on the Renumeration of Expert Witnesses* specifies the number of hours they expect will be needed for particular

48 https://www.parentassess.com/article/spotlight-on-the-short-parent-report

49 *Re G* [2006] 1 FLR 601; *Legal Aid Agency's Guidance on authorities and legal aid for cases in courts outside England and Wales* 1.7 paras 1 and 3.

pieces of work (benchmark hours) for ISW assessments and assessments of parent/s with learning difficulties. If the quote exceeds these hours it is advisable to make an application for prior authority to incur the costs. Work can be justified on assessment at the conclusion of the case, but this is a risky course of action. If the Legal Aid Agency refuses to pay the full amount, the solicitors firms acting for the legally aided parties have to pay the difference (unless the expert accepts the lower amount, by prior agreement or through negotiation).

Difficulties might arise in the case of a ParentAssess/CUBAS assessment that is conducted on parent(s) who do not have learning difficulties. The tailored approach taken in those assessments may mean that the hours undertaken for the work fall outside of the benchmark hours. The Legal Aid Agency may be reluctant to pay for a specialist assessment if it is not necessary. Consideration will need to be given to invite the local authority to meet any shortfall that is likely to arise.

The current rate for ISWs is based on the rates paid by Cafcass. In May 2022 Cafcass introduced a national rate of £35 per hour. ISW travel will be paid on the same basis as other experts i.e., at 2/3rds of the hourly rate.

Practice points

- Request a CV for the parenting assessor, even if a local authority is carrying out an assessment in house to ensure the assessor has the relevant skills and experience to undertake a tailored assessment of your particular client and any additional needs they may have.

- Identify who else will be contributing to the assessment other than the author of the report and request a CV for them.

- Submit a letter of instruction, even for a local authority in house assessment, to ensure that the assessment covers not only the standard assessment competencies but also any more tailored or nuanced aspects of the assessment that have to be addressed.

- Consider what are the "*real issues*" in the case.[50]

- Consider what challenges your client may face in particular types of assessments when considering their individual case e.g. a neuro divergent parent in a residential assessment unit (please see Chapter 4 parents with additional needs).

- Request a copy of any planning meeting minutes after the instruction of the parenting assessor and before your client moves into any placement/starts the assessment.

- Be sure to request a direction for regular logs for the placement as the assessment progresses, and ensure they are circulated. This is so you can address any concerns with your client at the time and build on any strengths.

- Arrange regular meetings with your client during the course of the assessment to check how they are coping with the assessment process.

Risk assessments

The Resolutions model/ approach been in place for a number of years although it is still not frequently use. It is a method of assessing risk in circumstances where carers maintain denial following findings made by the court that they have perpetrated injuries to their child.[51] That denial

---

50 *J (A Child) (Resolutions Model)* [2021] EWFC 58

51 *Working with denied child abuse: The Resolutions Approach* by Andrew Turnell and Susanne Essex; Child Abuse: *Rehabilitation without Admission – A New Way Forward*, Family Law, Dec 1999, Vol 29 by Gumbleton, J. and Lusk, A.

would exclude a parent from caring using other forms of standard assessment because they have not accepted their role in the harm.

In a Resolutions assessment, rather than seeking an admission from parents, the assessor works to create a safety/support network of family and/or friends who can supervise the parents with the children, minimising the risk. The assessment considers the *protective* rather than just *supportive* members of the network including their response to the court's findings. The support network is essential to the Resolutions' approach.

In *J (A Child) (Resolutions Model)* [2021] EWFC 58 HHJ Baker endorsed a reunification plan for a mother and child using the Resolutions Mode of parenting assessment. In previous proceedings the court made a finding that an older child had suffered an inflicted injury but could not conclude who caused the injury. The mother denied causing the injury but accepted the injury had been inflicted. The court considered what steps could be taken to safeguard the child despite that denial. The interplay between the Resolution's assessor, the social worker, the guardian, and the psychologist all led to a successful assessment and a detailed safety plan and roadmap were formulated. The court made a care order even though the child was to return to the mother's care, because of the risk and need to share parental responsibility, rather than to provide support.

Funding risk assessments

The Legal Aid Agency rate for specialist risk assessment expert services is set at £50.40 per hour. If an ISW is undertaking a risk assessment at a greater hourly rate than the ISW rate currently set at £35 an hour an application for prior authority will be needed.

The Legal Aid Agency needs to look at the nature of the work being done in each case to determine whether the social worker is providing independent social work services (the type of expert service most commonly required to be provided by a social worker in family proceedings) or whether they are providing specialist risk assessment expert services. *The Legal Aid Agency's Guidance on Remuneration Rates for Expert Services Determined as Risk Assessments*[52] sets out the criteria for paying the higher rate:

- The court has specified that a 'risk assessment' is required;
- The work being done is over and above that requiring ISW expertise, e.g.
    - there is a substantiated criminal allegation (such as a conviction for a sex offence or pending proceedings) relevant to the family case; and
    - a finding of sexual abuse relevant to the case has been made by a court.
- The report is specifically required to address the risk posed as a result of these factors.

See also *Legal Aid Agency Guidance on Renumeration of Expert Witnesses*, para 5.6 -5.11

Practice Points

- Identify the need for an assessment at the earliest opportunity. It is not a quick process and one that will not fit within the statutory 26-week timescale.

52 https://assets.publishing.service.gov.uk/media/5a7ef9ac40f0b62305b845a6/LAA-remuneration-rates-expert-services-determined-risk-assessments-guidance.pdf

- Are there sufficient family/friends to form a safety/support network?

- Is there a multi – agency approach from the professionals in the case?

- Is the person undertaking the assessment a specialist assessor and do they have the training, skills and experience to undertake the assessment?

- Are parents prepared to work in partnership with a number of professionals with a high level of monitoring and support?

- Do parents acknowledge that professionals have legitimate concerns?

- Are there positive aspects of the parent's care?

- If costs are to be apportioned between the parties' legal aid certificates, ensure there is a court order specifying that a 'risk assessment 'is required and the work is over and above that requiring independent social work expertise with the reasons why

Funding experts

Specific issues in relation to parenting and risk assessments are referred to above.

There are codified hourly rates for most, but not all experts.[53] A list of rates is appended to the Legal Aid Agency's *Guidance on the Renumeration of Expert Witnesses.* The rates differentiate between London and Non-

[53] The Civil Legal Aid (Remuneration) Regulations 2013

London experts. The address of the registered office determines where the expert is based, and the rate paid.

Where an expert discipline is not listed in the Remuneration Regulations, and there are no codified rates, the Legal Aid Agency will assess these costs on an individual basis. In those cases, you should consider applying to the Legal Aid Agency for prior authority to incur the costs before instructing the expert.

The Legal Aid Agency also set out in *Guidance on the Renumeration of Expert Witnesses* the number of hours they expect for particular pieces of work (benchmark hours) for a number of different experts, but not all.

If a quote exceeds the benchmark hours and/or hourly rates it is advisable to make an application for prior authority to incur the costs before instructing the expert. Work can be justified on assessment at the conclusion of the case, but this is a risky course of action as mentioned.

In care proceedings, experts are often single joint experts. Where the court gives a direction under *Family Procedure Rules 25.11(1)* for a single joint expert to be used, the court will also direct payment of the expert's fees and expenses.[54] Disbursements should be appropriately apportioned between parties (whether legally aid or not) where that is reasonable, e.g. in respect of a single joint expert. There may be some cases where apportionment is not appropriate (e.g. the local authority is instructing an ISW because it does not have an in-house assessor available to do the work within the court's timetable). If costs are not equally apportioned by the court, practitioners may want to apply for prior authority.[55] A direction in the order setting out the reason for any apportionment (or not) is helpful.

---

54 Family Procedure Rules 2010 r 25. 12 4(a)

55 Legal Aid Agency's *Guidance on authorities and legal aid for cases in courts Outside England and Wales.*

To complete a prior authority application for joint instruction of experts, one legal aid provider will need to make the application for prior authority on CCMS and give the certificate references of the other legally aided parties as part of the application.

The *Guidance on the Renumeration of Expert Witnesses* para 4 sets out additional provisions on expert witness funding including what is excluded.

CHAPTER FOUR

PARENTS WITH SPECIFIC NEEDS

The SRA requires solicitors to consider and take account of client's attributes, needs and circumstances.[1] Any legal professional working with clients should tailor their communications and provide a service that meets client's individual needs. Identifying a client's needs from the start of a case is vitally important to avoid miscommunication, which risks parents being prevented from engaging in proceedings and negative assumptions being made about them, all of which may lead to a breach of a parents' ECHR Article 6 and 8 rights.

A significant number of parents involved in care proceedings will have their own additional needs. Research from the Nuffield Family Justice Observatory found that a third of recent care cases in their sample involved parents with learning disabilities or difficulties.[2]

In *Re X and Y (Domestic Abuse: Participation Directions: Obligation to consider)* [2024] EWFC 121 (B), care proceedings before Mr Justice Williams, he stated:

> "*where a party is legally represented the obligation to consider how a party will participate fairly lies firstly, both temporally and procedurally, on the legal team. That is both good practice and I think in accordance with professional duties*".

---

1 SRA Code of Conduct for Solicitors, RELs and RFLs para 3.4

2 *Babies in care proceedings: What do we know about parents with learning disabilities or difficulties,* June 2024

Vulnerable witnesses

The *Family Procedure Rules Part 3A* supplemented by *Practice Direction 3AA* sets out the court's duties and powers in relation to helping parties whose ability to participate **or** to give evidence in family proceedings may be diminished by vulnerability, to ensure a fair hearing. It is important to distinguish participation and giving evidence.

These provisions are described as of "*fundamental importance to the administration of family justice*".[3]

The duties apply as soon as possible after the start of proceedings and continue until the resolution of the proceedings.[4] It is the duty of the court [5] **and** of all parties to the proceedings[6] to identify any party or witness who is a vulnerable person at the earliest possible stage of any family proceedings.[7] "*The Judge conducting the case management hearing at the start of care proceedings should as a matter of course investigate whether there are or maybe issues engaging Part 3A of the Rules and that the party's advocates should as far as practicable be in a position to respond*".[8]

The court has a duty to consider:

---

3 *Re S (vulnerable party: fairness of proceedings)* [2022] EWCA Civ8

4 Family Procedure Rules 2010 r 3A.9(1)

5 Family Procedure Rules 2010 r 1.1(2); 1.2 & 1.4 and Part 3A Family Procedure Rules

6 Family Procedure Rules 2010 r1.3

7 Family Procedure Rules 2010 PD 3AA 1.3

8 *Re S (vulnerable party: fairness of proceedings)* [2022] EWCA Civ8)

- Making participation directions for victims of domestic abuse.[9] A party or witness who is the victim/survivor of domestic abuse is automatically considered vulnerable.[10]

- Vulnerability of other parties or witnesses.[11]

The court must consider:

- Whether a party's participation in the proceedings (other than by giving evidence) is likely to be diminished by their vulnerability and, if so, whether it is necessary to make one or more participation directions.[12] Before making any participation directions, the court must consider any views expressed by the party about participating in the proceedings.[13]

- Whether the quality of evidence given by a party or witness is likely to be diminished by their vulnerability and, if so, whether it is necessary to make one or more participation directions.[14] Before making any participation directions, the court must consider any views expressed by the party or witness about giving evidence.[15]

"quality of evidence" means its quality in terms of completeness, coherence and accuracy; and for this purpose "coherence" refers to a

9 Family Procedure Rules 2010 r 3A.2A

10 Family Procedure Rules 2010 r 3A.2A, Practice Direction 3AA 2.2; Domestic Abuse Act 2021 section 63 (2)

11 Family Procedure Rules 2010 r 3A.3

12 Family Procedure Rules 2010 r 3A.4(1)

13 Family Procedure Rules 2010 r 3A.4(2)

14 Family Procedure Rules 2010 r 3A.5(1).

15 Family Procedure Rules 2010 r 3A.5(2)

witness's or a party's ability in giving evidence to give answers which address the questions put to the witness or the party and which can be understood both individually and collectively.[16]

What is a participation direction?

- A general case management direction made for the purpose of assisting a witness or party to give evidence or participate in proceedings; or

- A direction that a witness or party should have the assistance of one or more of the measures in rule 3A.8; "

The measures[17]:

- Prevent a party or witness from seeing another party or witness;

- Allow a party or witness to participate in hearings and give evidence by live link;

- Provide for a party or witness to use a device to help communicate;

- Provide for a party or witness to participate in proceedings with the assistance of an intermediary;

- Provide for a party or witness to be questioned in court with the assistance of an intermediary; or

- Do anything else which is set out in Practice Direction 3AA.

16 Family Procedure Rules 2010 r 3A.1

17 Family Procedure Rules 2010 3A.8 (1)

Participation directions are case specific and will be dependent on what is necessary in each case. Examples of participation directions for participation other than by way of giving evidence might be:

- The structure and the timing of the hearing
- The formality of language to be used in the court
- Using different routes in and out of the court building
- Using different waiting areas[18]
- Arrangements can be made for independent domestic abuse advisors (IDVAs) and independent sexual violence advisors (ISVA) at hearings[19]

Giving best evidence includes a party being able to effectively participate in expert assessments.[20]

When the court has decided that a vulnerable party, vulnerable witness or protected party should give evidence there shall be a 'ground rules hearing' before any hearing at which evidence is to be heard, where the court will consider any necessary participation directions.[21] This means considering making directions:

- As to the conduct of the advocates and the parties in respect of the evidence of that person; **and**,

18 Family Procedure Rules 2010 Practice Direction 3AA 4.2

19 Family Procedure Rules 2010 Practice Direction Practice Direction 27C

N (A Child), Re (Instruction of Expert) [2022] EWCA Civ 1588 (06 December 2022)

21 Family Procedure Rules 2010 Practice Direction 3AA 5.2

- to put any necessary support in place for that person.

The court will consider:

- The form of the evidence e.g. Oral evidence or sign language or other form of physical communication [22]

- The best way in which the person should give evidence, including considering whether the person's oral evidence should be given before the hearing, recorded and, if the court directs, transcribed, or given at the hearing with, if appropriate, participation directions being made.[23]

- In all cases in which it is proposed that a vulnerable party, vulnerable witness or protected party is to be cross-examined[24] the court must consider whether to make participation directions, including prescribing the manner in which the person is to be cross-examined. The court must consider whether to direct:

  (a) Any questions that can be asked by one advocate should not be repeated by another without the permission of the court;

  (b) Questions or topics to be put in cross-examination should be agreed before the hearing;

  (c) Questions to be put in cross-examination should be put by one legal representative or advocate alone, or, by the judge (if appropriate); and

---

22 Family Procedure Rules 2010 Practice Direction 3AA 5.3

23 Family Procedure Rules 2010 Practice Direction 3AA 5.4

24 Family Procedure Rules 2010 Practice Direction 3AA 5.5

(d) The taking of evidence should be managed in any other way.

Examples of participation directions for participation by way of giving evidence might be:

- Additional and/or different to any earlier participation directions so the measures to be used are not set in stone, and can be adapted as the case develops e.g. after written evidence has been filed (*D v R* [2023] EWHC 406 (Fam); *Re M:_Private law children proceedings: Case Management: Intimate Images* [2022] EWHC 986),

- The need for frequent breaks,

- The need for simple, direct questions, (and not several questions wrapped up in one) (*Re S (Vulnerable party: fairness of proceedings)* [2022] EWCA civ 8,

- A party not being visible to another party when giving oral evidence,

- The avoidance of unnecessarily intrusive questioning regarding traumatic experiences (*Re M:_Private law children proceedings: Case Management: Intimate Images* [2022] EWHC 986),

- Additional time allowed for asking questions of someone with a vulnerability,

- Separate waiting areas.

Where an expert e.g. psychologist/psychiatrist has been instructed to assess a vulnerable party, they should be asked in the letter of instruction to make recommendations about how a person can effectively participate in proceedings.

For intermediaries, please see below.

The court must also consider whether a vulnerable party, vulnerable witness or protected party has previously:

- Given evidence, and been cross-examined, in criminal proceedings and whether that evidence and cross-examination has been pre-recorded, or

- Given an interview which was recorded but not used in previous criminal or family proceedings.

- If so, the court should consider any available recordings being used in the family proceedings.

The ground rules hearing does not need to be separate to any hearing in the proceedings. Any hearing should include an intermediary if one is to be used.

The Advocates Gateway Toolkit 13[25] contains information about vulnerable witnesses in the family court, makes suggestions about how ground rules hearings can be effective and provides a ground rules checklist.[26]

Nothing in the rules gives the court power to direct that public funding must be available to provide a measure.[27]

---

25 https://www.theadvocatesgateway.org/_files/ugd/1074f0_48a0c6b6fca942fc819255e4104ac9de.pdf

26 https://www.theadvocatesgateway.org/_files/ugd/1074f0_395da62674464adbabfccc9e2fa43827.pdf

27 Family Procedure Rules 2010 r 3A.8 (4)

What must the court take into account when deciding whether to make a participation direction?

There is no definition of vulnerability, but the Family Procedure Rules set out what the court must take into account:

- The impact of any actual or perceived intimidation, including any behaviour towards the party or witness on the part of: a) any other party or other witness to the proceedings or members of the family or associates of that other party or other witness; or b) any members of the family of the party or witness;
- Whether the party or witness:
  a) suffers from mental disorder or otherwise has a significant impairment of intelligence or social function
  b) has a physical disability or suffers from a physical disorder; or
  c) is undergoing medical treatment;
- The nature and extent of the information before the court;
- The issues arising in the proceedings including (but not limited to) any concerns arising in relation to abuse;
- Whether a matter is contentious;
- The age, maturity and understanding of the party or witness;
- The social and cultural background and ethnic origins of the party or witness;
- The domestic circumstances and religious beliefs of the party or witness;

- Any questions which the court is putting to a witness in accordance with section 31g(6) of the Matrimonial and Family Proceedings Act 1984 Act;
- Any characteristic of the party or witness which is relevant to the participation direction;
- Measures available to the court;
- The costs of any available measure; and
- Any other matter set out in practice direction 3aa.

Abuse includes:

- Domestic abuse;
- Sexual abuse;
- Physical and emotional abuse;
- Racial and/or cultural abuse or discrimination;
- Forced marriage or so called "honour based violence";
- Female genital or other physical mutilation;
- Abuse or discrimination based on gender or sexual orientation; and
- Human trafficking.

Family Procedure Rules2010 Practice direction 3AA 2.1

Mrs Justice Theis DBE in *D v R* [2023] EWHC 406 (Fam) allowed an appeal against the outcome of a fact-finding hearing in a private law children case in which the judge had failed to comply with the court's duties under Part 3A and PD 3AA of the Family Procedure Rules 2010.Theis, J identified Mrs Justice Knowles' summary in *Re M (Private law children proceedings: case management: intimate images)* [2022] EWHC986 (Fam) as essential reading for any judge involved in proceedings with allegations of domestic abuse and as setting out a summary of the steps that a court should follow in these circumstances.

The court should consider the ability of the party or witness to:

- Understand the proceedings, and their role in them, when in court;
- Put their views to the court;
- Instruct their representative/s before, during and after the hearing; and
- Attend the hearing without significant distress.

Family Procedure Rules 2010 Practice Direction 3AA 3.10

Although the form C110A specifically asks the local authority whether there are any factors affecting a parent's ability to participate, we should not assume that the information provides a clear answer. Information may be contained in other evidence.[28]

The Advocates Gateway provides a helpful checklist Identifying vulnerability in witnesses and parties and making adjustments which can

28 *PQR (Supported Parenting For Learning Disabled Parents) (Rev 1)* [2018] EWFC B72

assist with direct screening questions.[29] The intermediary agency Communicourt has produced a guide to help practitioners in undertaking comprehension checks with clients, checking understanding and retention of information and asking questions going beyond a superficial "Do you understand?"[30]

Making an application for participation directions

An application can be made by:

- The local authority in section 4 of their application form C110A application for a care order[31];
- A C2 application during the proceedings[32];
- The court can make directions of its own initiative.[33]

Practice Points:

- An application should include why the party or witness would benefit from assistance [34] including:
    - Whether the party or witness falls within the assumption of vulnerability as a victim/survivor of domestic abuse;

https://www.theadvocatesgateway.org/_files/ugd/1074f0_bc65d21318414ba8a622a99723fdb2a0.pdf

30 Checking Understanding (communicourt.co.uk)

31 Family Procedure Rules 2010 r 3A.10 (1)

32 Family Procedure Rules 2010 r 3A.10 (1)

33 Family Procedure Rules 2010 r 3A.10 *(4)*

34 Family Procedure Rules 2010 Practice Direction 3AA 6.1

- The measures that would be likely to maximise the quality of evidence;

- Why the measures sought would be likely to improve the person's ability to participate in the proceedings; and

- Why the measure or measures sought would be likely to improve the quality of the person's evidence.

- The recommendations, where available, of any expert who has assessed the party or any intermediary assessment

- The Equal Treatment Bench Book, updated in July 2024[35], and its glossary of impairments, makes suggestions for reasonable adjustments and ideas for case preparation and the hearing for specific disabilities

- An assertion that party has a diagnosis with no supporting evidence of the diagnosis or the impact of the diagnosis in terms of the ability to participate will not be sufficient.[36]

Intermediaries

Intermediaries are not expert witnesses or witness supporters. They provide communication guidance and sit alongside the witness to monitor communication and intervene to assist with communication issues. They are officers of the court employed to be impartial not to advise and not to provide emotional support. An intermediary is different to a lay advocate (see below).

35 https://www.judiciary.uk/about-the-judiciary/diversity/equal-treatment-bench-book/

36 *Re X & Y (Intermediary: Practice and Procedure)* [2024] EWHC 906 (Fam)

The *Family Procedure Rules Part 3A.1* define an intermediary as a person whose function is to:

- Communicate questions put to a witness or party;
- Communicate to any person asking such questions the answers given by the witness or party in reply to them; and
- Explain such questions or answers so far as is necessary to enable them to be understood by the witness or party or the persons asking such questions.

Intermediaries may also make recommendations about and assist with the use of communication aids, stress reduction strategies to assist with regulation of behaviour and emotions.

A failure to allow a party to give evidence with the support of an intermediary where one has been found to be necessary is likely to amount to a fundamental breach of a party's Article 6 rights to a fair hearing.

In *Re N (A Child)* [2019] EWCA CIV 1997 King, LJ said:

> "*in my judgement it would go too far to say that a rehearing is inevitable in all cases where there has been a failure to identify a party as vulnerable with the consequence that no ground rules have been in place in preparation for their giving evidence and no intermediary or other special measures provided for their assistance, but the necessity for there to be a fair trial must be at the forefront of the Judge's mind. Being such as case, whether there should be a retrial must depend upon all the circumstances of the case, not only or principally upon the likely outcome of a rehearing* "

There have been two recent important cases regarding the use of intermediaries.

West Northamptonshire Council v KA & Ors [2024] EWHC 79 (Fam) Mrs Justice Lieven at first instance gave guidance whilst noting that the *Family Procedure Rules* provide a definition of an intermediary but otherwise give no guidance on the appointment or role of an intermediary. She looked to the criminal law applying the same tests for intermediary applications currently used in criminal proceedings:

- Intermediaries should be used in *"rare"* cases during a court user's evidence, and in *"exceptionally rare"* cases, throughout proceedings.

- An intermediary should only be used where there is a *"compelling reason"*, and the court is unable to make sufficient adjustments in the absence of an intermediary

- An intermediary should not be appointed simply because the process "*would be improved*" *R v Cox* [2012] EWCA crim 549.

- The first and usual approach is for the judge and the lawyers to ensure that simple language is used, and breaks taken to ensure that litigants understand what is happening.

- All advocates in cases involving vulnerable parties or witnesses should be familiar with the Advocates Gateway and the advice on how to help vulnerable parties understand and participate in the proceedings.

- It is the role of the judge to consider whether the appointment of an intermediary is justified. It may often be the case that all the parties support the appointment, because it will make the hearing easier, but that is not the test the judge needs to apply nor is the recommendation from an expert determinative.

- Although there are obvious and important differences between family court cases and those involving criminal charges, the reasons for the appointment of intermediaries and their function in assisting those with communication difficulties facing important litigation, are essentially the same.

- Intermediaries are appointed, whether in criminal or family cases, to ensure that the individual in question can participate in the proceedings so that their fair trial rights are protected.

- The guidance of the Court of Appeal in *R v Thomas (Dean)* is applicable to the consideration of the same issues in the family justice system, albeit the court will need to have close regard to the nature of the case and the evidence that the individual needs to engage with.

In *Re X & Y (Intermediary: Practice and Procedure)* [2024] EWHC 906 (Fam) Mr Justice Williams also at first instance endorsed the guidance provided by Lieven, J and:

- Clarified that the test for an appointment of an intermediary is "*necessary*" rather than "*compelling*" as required under *Family Procedure Rules 3A.2A(3), 3A.4(1)* and *3A.5(1).*

- Whether that means that 'nothing else will do' would require consideration of the other means by which fair participation can be achieved.

- The test remains a strict one although what is necessary will bear some correlation to the measure proposed. " *The necessity of a direction for a screen or a break is likely to be much easier to demonstrate than a direction for an intermediary".*

- Evidence of necessity may come from various sources for example experts' reports, medical history, information from the social worker, from the party's legal team that even by deployment of all their skills as solicitor and counsel using the Advocates

Toolkits, they do not consider the party or witness can participate fairly without an intermediary.

- Ultimately the court is engaged in an evaluation of what participation directions are necessary to ensure that a 'fair hearing' is achieved either in relation to a witness' evidence or to a party's participation in the proceedings.

- It should not be the default position that a witness or party who is identified as vulnerable and needing measures to be taken to support their participation or giving of evidence requires an intermediary.

- *"A major component of the role of legal representatives (solicitor and counsel) is to ensure their client understands the proceedings and their role in them, putting their views to the court, ensuring their client is able to give them instructions in advance of court and in court and enabling them to attend court without significant distress. Only if the court is satisfied that the usual support a legal team (adopting the use of the tools available) and other measures available to the court will not enable the party to participate fairly will it be necessary to provide for an intermediary".*

- An application for an intermediary assessment or the appointment of an intermediary is not made under *Part 25 Family Procedure Rules 2010* as it is not an expert assessment. It is a case management direction. A *Part 18* application is the correct process.

Funding intermediaries

The cost of funding an intermediary in court falls on HMCTS. A direction must be obtained for each hearing at which an intermediary is required.

There are two types of HMCTS approved intermediary service:

- Managed and approved service providers (MASPs) larger organisations with intermediary services available nationally. These are currently:

    a) Communicourt

    b) The Intermediary Cooperative (TIC)

    c) Triangle for Children and Young People up until the age of 30

- Approved service providers (ASPs) are self-employed individuals who provide specialist intermediary services. These include:

    a) Aspire Social Work Intermediary Services with named individuals.

    b) Named individuals (expected to give their location, areas of law, age groups, specialisms or interests.

There may be occasions when it is not possible to book an approved provider e.g. when the client is already supported by a non-approved provider. For services funded by HMCTS you must ask for permission to use a non-approved provider by emailing HMCTScontracted services@justice.gov.uk.

Beware of the risks of using non-approved intermediaries. In *A Local Authority v Mother & Ors* [2021] EWHC 2794 (Fam) Mrs Justice Lieven determined that a costs order against one intermediary was justified after a final hearing collapsed when the individual who attended the hearing to act as an intermediary for a party was not competent to fulfil the role.

For services funded by the Legal Aid Agency, an application will need to be made for prior authority. Legal aid funding can be provided for an intermediary/lay advocate to be used for communication between a practitioner and their client away from the court room, subject to the Legal Aid Agency being satisfied that it is justifiable and reasonable.[37]

<u>Practice points:</u>

- If there any concerns about a party's ability to communicate, consideration should be given to an intermediary assessment as soon as possible. The waiting times for an assessment are approximately two – three weeks once permission has been given by the court and reports can be completed within five working days.

- Consider what measures, other than an intermediary, could be put in place to support the client.

- Should a second person (e.g. a lay advocate, representative from solicitors offices) be at court with the client to implement any strategies which support the client's participation, particularly if permission is not given for an intermediary for hearings? For example, in a hearing the client will be sat behind their advocate, who will be taking a note or be on their feet, making it difficult to be able to focus on the client's presentation, checking they are following proceedings, or be able to answer any questions the client might have.

Lay advocates

Re C (Lay Advocates) (2) [2020] EWHC1762 (Fam) Keehan J:

> "*The term lay advocate for the purposes of this judgment means a person who is qualified and has experience of assisting and supporting a party in proceedings who has an intellectual impairment or learning difficulties which compromises their*

[37] *Legal Aid Agency Guidance on the Remuneration of Expert Witnesses* paragraph 5.33 and 5.34

> *ability to process and comprehend information given to them. The function of the lay advocate is to ensure that the party does understand the information provided and is able to respond to the same and thereby, isn't able to participate affectively in the proceedings. This assistance and support will be required both in court during the proceedings and out of court for the purposes of taking instructions and preparing the parties case for the court proceedings".*

The judge clarified the role for a lay advocate and funding responsibilities:

- A lay advocate does not provide legal services.
- A lay advocate is not a McKenzie Friend.
- A lay advocate is not an intermediary (albeit an individual may be qualified to act as an intermediary and as well as a lay advocate).

Research shows that parental advocacy services have helped provide parents across the board with a voice during child protection processes, including improving relationships between social workers and parents, improved communication.[38]

Funding a lay advocate

Legal aid is available to fund a lay advocate to be used for communication between a practitioner and their client away from the court room subject

[38] *The Power of Parental Advocacy*, NYAS Cymru https://nyas.s3.eu-west-1.amazonaws.com/GetSupport/SupportingFamilies/NYAS-Parent-Advocacy-Research-Report_Caitlin%20Evans.pdf

to the Legal Aid Agency being satisfied that it is a justifiable and reasonable disbursement.[39]

In *Re C* The Secretary of State for Justice appeared before Keehan, J and agreed on behalf of HMCTS that payment for lay advocates at hearings is a matter for HMCTS and funding to assist with communication between the client and solicitor is a matter for the Legal Aid Agency.

Deaf parents

There are 18 million adults in the UK who are deaf or have hearing loss or tinnitus. That equates to one in three adults. An estimated 1.2 million adults in the UK have hearing loss severe enough that they would not be able to hear most conversational speech.[40]

There is no consensus on the total number of British Sign Language (BSL) users or deaf BSL users in the UK. The 2021 Census Data for England and Wales reports 22,000 people who use British Sign Language as their main language in England and Wales. The total number of people in the UK who use British Sign Language (not necessarily as their main language) is estimated to be 151,000 and of these 87,000 are deaf (British Deaf Association). BSL is the preferred language of over 87,000 deaf people in the UK for whom English may be a second or third language. That means a person's first language is BSL not English. There is a common misconception that deaf people can access information through lipreading people's speech or by reading written English.[41]

---

39 *Legal Aid Agency Guidance on the Remuneration of Expert Witnesses* 5.34

40 RNID Prevalence of deafness and hearing loss 17 July 2024 https://rnid.org.uk/get-involved/research-and-policy/facts-and-figures/prevalence-of-deafness-and-hearing-loss/

41 *A & B (Children) (deaf parent – assessment and practice)* [2021] EWFC 10

The British Deaf Association has produced a helpful resource on sign language, communicating with deaf people and working with interpreters.[42]

Lawyers acting for a parent with a hearing disability have a duty to identify that as a feature of the case at the earliest opportunity. The court needs to consider the issue including any support required and the funding of that support at the first CMH with the aim of giving clear and detailed directions.[43]

In *Re C (A Child)* [2014] EWCA Civ 128 the President of the Family Division gave guidance:

- It is the duty of those who are acting for a parent who has a hearing disability to identify that as a feature of the case at the earliest opportunity.

- Both those acting for a parent and those acting for the local authority should make the issue known to the court when proceedings are issued.

- Expert advice on the impact of the deaf person's disability should be addressed at the case management hearing. An application for expert involvement should be the subject of a properly constituted application for leave to instruct the expert under *Part 25* of the *Family Procedure Rules 2010.*

- Communication between a profoundly deaf individual and professionals for the purpose of assessment and court proceedings involves a sophisticated, and to a degree bespoke understanding of both the process of such communication and the level and

---

42 https://bda.org.uk/help-resources/#communicating

43 *Re Y (A Child) (Leave to oppose adoption)* [2020] EWCA CIV 1287

character of the deaf person's comprehension of the issues which those in the hearing population simply take as commonplace.

- There are differences between British Sign Language and English Supported Sign Language. Different people from the population who have a hearing disability will use one or both or neither; they may have their own individual way of communication.

- Deaf Relay Interpretation is undertaken by a deaf person who acts as an "intermediary" between the qualified sign language interpreter and the deaf person to provide a specialist service and approach the communication with the deaf person from a deaf perspective, "*breaking down issues and providing, what one report we have read refers to as, 'cultural brokerage*".

- The court, the local authority and Cafcass must all function within the terms of the Equality Act 2010.

In *A & B (Children) (deaf parent – assessment and practice)* [2021] EWFC 10 Elizabeth Isaacs QC, sitting as a deputy High Court judge reflected on how the specific lessons from this case might be of wider interest in future similar cases given the unusually limited number of reported cases dealing with deaf parents in public law proceedings. It is essential reading for practitioners working with deaf parents. Whereas *Re C* primarily considered the way in which reasonable adjustments should be made during court proceedings, *A & B* considered the obligations of the local authority as well. The local authority failed to understand the mother's needs as a deaf parent throughout the case including failure to provide lip speakers during contact sessions and LAC meetings. It was held that:

- The mother should be treated as a person with a disability due to her deafness. She was also to be treated as disabled for the purpose of the *Equality Act 2010* section 6;

- The *Equality Act 2010 section 20* places a duty on public bodies to take reasonable steps and to make reasonable adjustments to avoid placing a disabled person at a substantial disadvantage. This can include ensuring that necessary information is provided to the disabled person in an accessible format. The duty also requires the court to take reasonable steps to ensure that a disabled parent can participate effectively and fairly in the proceedings.

- Guidance in the Equal Treatment Bench Book highlights the practical ways in which reasonable adjustments should be made by the court.

- The court was also referred to the Advocates Gateway Toolkit 11 "*planning to question someone who is deaf*"[44];

- It was consistent with the court's duty to ensure accessibility of information, the judge prepared a simplified version of the judgment, which was read aloud to the mother at the conclusion of the hearing with the help of the lip-speakers and the intermediary;

- Professionals working with a deaf parent need to be 'deaf-aware', including the contact supervisor and the foster carer (who was providing information to the mother);

- A specialist consultant clinical psychologist for deaf people, defined two key elements to being 'deaf aware'

---

https://www.theadvocatesgateway.org/_files/ugd/1074f0_962a7d479ee94bb295d3300cc46cb8c5.pdf

a) Having the ability to notice any communication breakdown and adapting to ensure that the communication with the deaf person works, and

b) being aware that the deaf person may have knowledge gaps, not because they are necessarily learning disabled, but because they have missed communication.

- In every case involving a deaf parent, a cognitive and capacity assessment should be undertaken at the outset of the proceedings by a psychologist with specialist experience in the assessment of deaf adults;

- A specialist cognitive assessment is essential in order to understand the way that the parent communicates so that reasonable adjustments can be made by both the local authority and the court;

- A specialist parenting assessment by an expert in deafness is required.

- It is necessary to follow specialist advice as to how best to facilitate communication;

- The social work evidence template SWET paragraph 10 '*statement of procedural fairness' have the contents of this statement been communicated to mother, father, significant others and the child in a way which can be clearly understood? If not, what has been tried?* Should be responded to in full;

- The mother's disability as a deaf parent should have been accurately recorded by the court as she was wrongly identified as hearing impaired on most orders;

- There should have been a 'joined-up' approach between adult services and children's services before the child was born, to identify the mother's needs as a deaf parent;

- Using the father to communicate with mother was not appropriate for matters of substance.

British Sign Language

Sign languages differ significantly from spoken language. They are whole body languages. BSL is a visual-gestural language with a distinct grammar using handshakes, facial expressions, gesture and body language to convey meaning.

Sign language is not the same internationally. There are variations as expected in different spoken languages. For example, in the UK, Ireland and the USA, the main spoken language is English but all three have separate sign language.

There are different sign languages worldwide and different regional dialects. However, there is a collection of internationally accepted signs, International Sign (IS).

Funding BSL signers

The Legal Aid Agency have set their hourly rate for BSL signers at £57.60 for out of London and £32.80 in London. There are insufficient BSL signers nationwide, fewer who are accredited and even fewer still who will work at Legal Aid Agency rates. An application for prior authority to incur the costs will be necessary for costs outside of Legal Aid Agency rates.

Deaf intermediaries

There are very few deaf intermediaries in the country. They are in high demand.

The shortage of deaf intermediaries and interpreters creates significant issues when listing hearings because their availability is limited. However, their attendance is critical.

In *West Northamptonshire Council v KA & Ors* [2024] EWHC 79 (Fam) Lieven, J accepted the appointment of a deaf intermediary for the mother was necessary for the entirety of the hearing. The issues went beyond the fact that she was profoundly deaf and included wider communication difficulties. The judge highlighted the problem with the use of a hearing intermediary for a person who is deaf, given the very specific interpretation issues involved with BSL.

Parents with learning disabilities or difficulties

Public Health England Definitions:

Learning disability

> "*A significantly reduced ability to understand new or complex information, to learn new skills (impaired intelligence), with a reduced ability to cope independently (impaired social functioning), which started before adulthood*"

Learning difficulty

> "*A reduced intellectual ability for a specific form of learning and includes conditions such as dyslexia (reading), dyspraxia (affecting physical co-ordination) and attention deficit hyperactivity disorder (ADHD)*"

These definitions are not connected to parenting.

In June 2024 Nuffield Family Justice Observatory published research *Babies in Care Proceedings: What do we know about parents with learning disabilities or difficulties*[45] completed by the Institute of Public Care, Oxford Brookes University. The research looked at the prevalence, circumstances and experiences of parents with learning disabilities whose babies were the subject of care proceedings from their referral to children's services until the conclusion of proceedings.

The study found one in three parents at risk of having their babies removed from their care had learning disabilities or difficulties. In approximately three quarters of cases the parents learning disability or difficulty was not identified until court proceedings were underway.

Late identification means that pre-proceedings assessments, support and communication would not be tailored to a parents' needs with a risk that parents did not understand what was happening.

The then President of the Family Division Sir James Munby issued Practice Guidance in 2018 *Family Proceedings: Parents with a Learning Disability*[46] this was primarily to draw attention to *Good practice guidance on working with parents with a learning disability* issued by the Working Together with Parents Network and the Norah Fry Centre. It has subsequently been updated.[47]

The good practice guidance is essential reading for practitioners working with parents with learning disabilities and difficulties. It sets out five features of good practice:

- Accessible information and communication;

---

45 https://www.nuffieldfjo.org.uk/resource/babies-in-care-proceedings-what-do-we-know-about-parents-with-learning-disabilities-or-difficulties

46 https://www.judiciary.uk/guidance-and-resources/family-proceedings-parents-with-a-learning-disability/

https://childhub.org/sites/default/files/library/attachments/FINAL-2021-WTPN-UPDATE-OF-THE-GPG.pdf

- Clear and co-ordinated referral and assessment processes and eligibility criteria;
- Support designed to meet the needs of parents and children based on assessment of their needs and strengths;
- Long-term support, if necessary; and,
- Access to independent advocacy.

At the invitation of the Official Solicitor, Mrs Justice Knowles concluded her judgment in *Re H* [2022] EWFC 10 with learning points for care cases where a parent has a learning disability:

- *Good Practice Guidance on Working with Parents with a Learning Disability which* should be more widely disseminated to both children and family social workers and adult social care workers. The guidance should also be at the forefront of local authority planning. Social workers involved in cases with a parent with learning disabilities should, as a matter of good practice, be capable of demonstrating that the guidance has been taken into account in any care planning or proposals put forward by a local authority.
- There must be timely referrals to adult social care for a parent with learning difficulties, in their own right.
- A learning disabled parent involved with children's social care must be given:

  (a) A document setting out what support is available to them in their own right, how often it is available, the time-scales for its availability and who is responsible for its delivery; and

(b) A document setting out what support is available to them with the care of their child, how often it is available, the time- scales for its availability and who is responsible for its delivery.

Both documents must be shared with children's and adult social care as part of the joined- up thinking and planning that is required in these cases.

Working Together with Parents Network has produced top tips for working with parents with learning difficulties or disabilities.[48]

The Advocates Gateway has another helpful tool kit *Planning to question someone with a learning disability*[49] with good practice and tips useful outside of an advocacy setting including how learning disability can affect communication, making sure you are understood and making sure you understand.

Cognitive assessments

A cognitive assessment builds a picture of someone's strengths and weaknesses in specific areas e.g. how parents process oral and written information, attention, memory etc.

An early cognitive assessment is helpful. It can:

- inform practitioners and the local authority's communication with a parent
- help a parent access support

48 Top tips (bristol.ac.uk).

https://www.theadvocatesgateway.org/_files/ugd/1074f0_f2452243bb7c419b9e5e0b47edce378e.pdf

- inform other assessments
- inform decisions regarding a parent's capacity to understand legal proceedings, make informed decisions, and effectively participate in their case

In *West Northamptonshire Council v The Mother (Psychological Assessments)* [2024] EWHC 395 (Fam) a first instance decision, Mrs Justice Lieven dismissed an application for a cognitive assessment by a psychologist but gave guidance on when applications for a psychologist to undertake a cognitive assessment in care proceedings should be made and the approach that the family court should take.

There was nothing in the local authority's threshold document or initial SWET to suggest the mother had any cognitive impairment or significant communication difficulties or that she has any special educational needs. The application for the assessment had been made before the solicitor had met the client, on the basis of what counsel had reported back after discussions at the first hearing when there had been discussion about the local authority using a ParentAssess framework.

The judge set out:

- An application under Part 25 for a psychological/cognitive assessment must be accompanied by proper evidence which explains why the case goes beyond the standard difficulties faced by many parents in care proceedings.
- The evidence must explain why the parent's needs cannot be properly managed by careful use of language and the professionals taking the time to explain matters in an appropriate manner.
- The evidence must address why such an assessment is "*necessary*".

The judge's view was it would often be the case that if a parent does have cognitive issues this will have been identified at school, during previous interactions with the local authority and/or in pre-proceedings work. As we know from the Nuffield Family Justice Observatory research (*Babies in Care Proceedings: What do we know about parents with learning disabilities or difficulties*), discussed above, that is not always the case. It will not be possible to identify the nature and extent of any difficulties without an assessment that have gone unrecognised. It may be difficult to get funding for a lay advocate or other advocacy support without a cognitive assessment.

<u>Parenting assessments</u>

Tailored and appropriate assessments should be undertaken (*Re C (Care Proceedings: Parents with Disabilities)* [2014] EWCA Civ 128 T).

For parents with learning disabilities or learning difficulties (or other additional needs) an assessment using the ParentAssess or CUBAS framework should be undertaken. Alternatively for residential assessments, consider using a specialist unit such as Symbol.

Please see Chapter 3 parenting assessments.

<u>Support</u>

Parents should receive support in their own right.

In *Re D (A Child) (No 3)* [2016] EWFC 1 the President of the Family Division referred to an extract from the judgment of Gillen J in *Re G and A (Care Order: Freeing Order: Parents with a Learning Disability*) [2006] NIFam 8:

> "*Children of parents with learning difficulties often do not enter the child protection system as the result of abuse by their parents. More regularly the prevailing concerns centre on a perceived risk of neglect, both as the result of the parents' intellectual*

> *impairments, and the impact of the social and economic deprivation commonly faced by adults with learning difficulties. It is in this context that a shift must be made from the old assumption that adults with learning difficulties could not parent to a process of questioning why appropriate levels of support are not provided to them so that they can parent successfully and why their children should often be taken into care. At its simplest, this means a court carefully inquiring as to what support is needed to enable parents to show whether or not they can become good enough parents rather than automatically assuming that they are destined to fail. The concept of "parenting with support" must move from the margins to the mainstream in court determinations*"

Research conducted by Nadine Tilbury and Beth Tarleton (2023) "*Substituted parenting: What does this mean for parents with learning disabilities in the family court context?*"[50] considers the term "substituted parenting". This can be used by local authorities as a negative concept in cases in which the support they have identified as necessary is extensive with the high level of support required equating to 'substituted parenting' – said, by local authorities, to be detrimental, as it confuses children as to who their parent is. The 'tipping point' between what is extensive and what is excessive, and whether the proposed support amounted to 'substituted parenting', was not fixed. Rather, it was felt to be dependent on the individual judge or case. The research is an important read if a practitioner is putting forward a case on behalf of a parent to counter a local authority's position that support is excessive.

In *Re H (Parents With Learning Difficulties: Risk of Harm)* [2023] EWCA Civ 59, the Court of Appeal set out the need for an analysis and exploration of options in such situations and said that it cannot be

50 https://www.bristol.ac.uk/media-library/sites/sps/documents/wtpn/SP%20Report.pdf

concluded that support is adverse to the child without scrutinising the care plan. It is necessary to deal with the following:

- Identify which specific elements of the support package are potentially problematic (for example level of support, nature of support, physical aspects of parenting, assumed attachment issues);
- Assess the likelihood and impact of the risk in relation to each specific element
- Identify options to address / reduce / eliminate / manage each of the identified risks;
- Trial the options, where possible. The analysis should not be conducted as a generic, theoretical exercise;
- A judge must be rigorous in exploring and probing the local authority's thinking in cases where it may be affected by resource issues;
- Support for parents with learning difficulties may have to be long-term, extending throughout the child's minority;
- *"in the interests of the child, the starting point should have been, first, to identify and describe the level of support needed by the family, secondly ascertain what can and should be being done under the local authority's obligations, and thirdly to determine whether, with that in place, the child's welfare needs will be met. This involves a careful assessment of what the package would look like, how practical it is and how intrusive it would be for the child".*

Care Act assessments for parents and carers

The threshold for an assessment of need by social services under *Care Act 2014 section 9* is a low one. There just needs to be an appearance to the local authority that an individual may have needs for care and support.

An assessment will involve considering the eligibility criteria in the *Care and Support (Eligibility Criteria) Regulations 2015, Regulation 2* which include criteria such as maintaining a habitable home environment, budgeting, accessing work and developing personal relationships. Only one of the criteria relates to carrying out any caring responsibilities for a child. If there is evidence from family members and professionals that an individual may need Regulation 2 support, this can be presented to the local authority when asking the local authority to progress an assessment under s.9 of the Care Act 2014.

An adult's needs meet the eligibility criteria if[51]:

- The adult's needs arise from or are related to a physical or mental impairment or illness;
- As a result of the adult's needs the adult is unable to achieve two or more of the specified outcomes; and,
- As a consequence there is, or is likely to be, a significant impact on the adult's well-being.

In addition, the statutory guidance[52] is a useful tool as to how person centred care and support planning should work under the Care Act. The process is supposed to be flexible and can be adapted to best fit with the person's needs, wishes and goals. The local authority should also consider

---

51 Regulation 2 of the Care and Support (Eligibility Criteria) Regulation 2015

52 *Care and Support Statutory Guidance*

the individual's own strengths. As the guidance makes clear [53] the purpose of the assessment is to identify an individual's needs and how these impact on their well-being, and the outcomes that the person wishes to achieve in their day to day life.

Of particular relevance for family cases may be paragraph 6.65 of the Code which makes it clear that there should be a whole family approach to take a holistic view of the person's needs and to identify how the adult's needs for care and support impact on family members or others in the support network.

Following the assessment process, a care and support plan should be drawn up and the availability of direct payments should be identified too. However, it is important to note that a direct payment may not be an option in certain circumstances, such as where there is a court order for a drug or alcohol treatment programme.

Once a care and support plan is drawn up there should be a review of the plan no later than every twelve months, although a light touch review should be considered 6 – 8 weeks after agreement and sign off of the plan and budget.

Neurodivergent parents

> *"Neurodiversity describes the population as a whole and recognises the diversity of different brains. Neurotypical describes most of the population the majority group that expresses themselves in ways that are seen as the societal "norm". Neurodivergent describes the minority group that diverts neurologically from said "norm". This is estimated to be 1 in 7*

---

53 *paragraph 6.9 Care and Support Statutory Guidance*

people, although with an increase in awareness and late diagnosis this in likely to be higher" NHS England[54])

Types of neurodivergence include:

- Autism/Autism Spectrum Condition (ASC) / Autism Spectrum Disorder (ASD)
- Attention Deficit Hyperactivity Disorder (ADHD) / Variable Attention Stimulus Trait (VAST)
- Dyspraxia
- Dyslexia
- Dysgraphia
- Dyscalculia
- Tourette's Syndrome (TS)

Autistic parents

In research undertaken with legal professionals 19% of practitioners believed autism to be an extremely rare condition.[55] However, The National Autistic Society estimate that 1 in 100 people have autism.

---

54 https://www.hee.nhs.uk/our-work/pharmacy/transforming/initial/foundation/resources/edi/neurodiversity#:~:text=Neurodivergent%20describes%20the%20minority%20group,in%20likely%20to%20be%20higher.

55 *Legal professionals' knowledge and experience of autistic adults in the family justice system.* George, R., Crane, L., Bingham, R., Pophale, C., & Remington, A. (2018) Journal of Social Welfare and Family Law, 40(1), 78-97).

Autism is not an illness, disorder or mental health condition. It is a neurodevelopmental difference, from birth.

The 'core characteristics' of autism, which must be present (and must have been present throughout a person's life) for an autism diagnosis to be made are:

- Communication and social interaction differences; and
- Restricted and repetitive behaviours and interests (often referred to by autistic people as self-soothing or self-regulating behaviours, and focused and dedicated interests), including sensory differences·

  National Autistic Society[56]

People on the autistic spectrum vary greatly in their abilities, challenges and preferences.

Research exploring the experiences of autistic adults who had experience of the family justice system showed significant misunderstandings about autism, and a system which struggled to make appropriate adjustments which would allow autistic court users to have access to justice on an equivalent basis to non-autistic litigant.[57]

The case of *D and E (Parent with Autism)* [2020] EWFC B18 gives a comprehensive overview of the difficulties which a parent with Autistic Spectrum Condition might encounter and how the court system can make reasonable adjustments. It is essential reading for any practitioner

---

56 https://www.autism.org.uk/advice-and-guidance/topics/diagnosis/assessment-and-diagnosis/criteria-and-tools-used-in-an-autism-assessment)

57 *Our normal is different: autistic adults' experiences of the family courts*, George, R, Crane, L and Remington, 2020

57 *Our normal is different: autistic adults' experiences of the family courts*, George, R, Crane, L and Remington, 2020

working with an autistic parent reaffirming the importance of recognising the individuality of parents and the need for tailored support in parenting assessments and care arrangements.

The judge made suggestions for reasonable adjustments whilst recognising every autistic person is different:

- Giving very explicit instructions on all case management directions;
- Aiming to keep the same judge in all preliminary hearings;
- Explaining in advance what the hearing procedure will be like;
- Providing a written time-table;
- Explaining that the party can visit the hearing venue in advance to look around;
- Reducing anxiety by reserving a private waiting/conference room for use by the autistic person and telling the party that this will be arranged;
- Preparing a simple chronology of dates which are personal to the individual as reference points;
- Explaining the procedure at the outset of the hearing including the length and timing of breaks;
- Providing regular breaks, such as 10-minute breaks after every 60 minutes in court to prevent anxiety escalating and other symptoms developing as a result;

- Arranging appropriate seating: asking the person where they would like to sit such as a preference to sit near a door as an escape route;

- Preventing people going in and out the room or moving behind the individual;

- Switching off lights, fans and heaters with any humming sound, however quiet, allowing the party to wear sunglasses or a hat and use of window blinds;

- Establishing ground rules at the outset in terms of appropriate styles of questioning;

- Avoiding figurative communication, such as 'take a seat';

- Avoiding hypothetical questions, both regarding the substance of the person's evidence and regarding court procedure;

- Avoiding legal jargon.

Guidance is also provided in the Equal Treatment Bench Book.

The Advocacy Gateway Toolkit 3 *Planning to question someone with autism*[58] includes the impact of autism on communication Toolkit 15 *Witnesses and defendants with autism: memory and sensory issues.*[59]

---

https://www.theadvocatesgateway.org/_files/ugd/1074f0_aee057da809d412f88afd683dcc402e7.pdf

https://www.theadvocatesgateway.org/_files/ugd/1074f0_5aeb50cd277f4f5094bbe5b8a989b3bc.pdf

Family Law Advice for the Neurodivergent Community (FLANC)[60] has an excellent set of resources for clients and professionals including guides to autism for lawyers, court staff and judges.

Assessments

Any assessments identifying a parents' needs should be obtained as soon as possible. They will give a context for behaviours.

The case of *D and E* highlights the importance of an appropriate targeted assessment with an assessor with the correct skill set. The outcome of an assessment in proceedings was very different from the conclusions reached in the initial assessment where no adjustments had been made to support the mother. Many of the features of the mother's presentation which had given rise to local authority concerns were features of her diagnosis.

It is important that any letter of instruction gives information on the neurotype of the parent.

The Department of Education have produced *A manual for good social work practice Supporting Adults who have autism* which is helpful in identifying "*..the very practical and sometimes complicated issues that they [social workers] need to know about for practice with adults who have autism*".[61]

Parenting assessments

Consider the appropriate parenting assessment for your client.

60 https://flanc.org.uk/for-professionals/

61 https://assets.publishing.service.gov.uk/media/5a806deaed915d74e622e664/Pt1_Autism_Learning_Materials_Accessible.pdf.

Residential assessments may have additional challenges for an autistic parent e.g. shared facilities, noisy environments, socialising with other residents.

Support

Support should be tailored. Often support services are generic. It is important that any referral gives information on the neurotype of the parent.

Mental ill health

The Advocates Gateway Toolkit 12 deals with *Planning to question someone with a suspected (or diagnosed) mental health disorder.*[62] It includes potential questions for an expert assessment as well as practical tips on asking questions.

The Family Justice Council has produced practical guidance on working with clients at risk of suicide.[63]

English not as a first or primary language

A witness statement must comply with the requirements set out in the *Practice Direction 22A (Family Procedure Rules Part 22.4 (2)).*

Where the affidavit/statement is in a foreign language the party wishing to rely on it must[64]:

62 https://www.theadvocatesgateway.org/_files/ugd/1074f0_a1f896d74e30440f9ec8bac9ab27f642.pd

63 https://www.judiciary.uk/wp-content/uploads/2023/10/At-Risk-of-Suicide-Information-for-professionals-working-within-the-court-system-FJC.pdf

64 Family Procedure Rules Practice Direction 22A 8.2

- have it translated; and
- must file the foreign language affidavit/statement with the court; and
- the translator must sign the translation to certify that it is accurate.

Where a witness statement or affidavit does not comply with *Part 22* or the Practice Direction in relation to its form, the court may refuse to admit it as evidence and may refuse to allow the costs arising from its preparation.[65]

In *NN v ZZ & Ors* [2013] EWHC 2261 (Fam) Mr Justice Peter Jackson (as he then was) in a postscript to his judgment set out principles as to how evidence from non-English speakers should be obtained, emphasizing the importance of following proper procedures, to ensure fairness and clarity in the proceedings:

- An affidavit or statement by a non-English speaking witness must be prepared in the witness's own language *before* being translated into English. This is implicit from *Practice Direction 22A* of the *Family Procedure Rules 2010, paragraph 8.2.*
- There must be clarity about the process by which a statement has been created. In all cases, the statement should contain an explanation of the process by which it has been taken, for example, face to face, over the telephone, by Skype or based on a document written in the witness's own language.

65 Family Procedure Rules Part 22 14.1

- If a solicitor has been instructed by the litigant, s/he should be fully involved in the process and should not subcontract it to the client.

- If presented with the statement in English from a witness who cannot read or speak English, the solicitor should question its provenance and not simply use the document as a proof of evidence.

- The witness should be spoken to wherever possible, using an interpreter, and a draft statement should be prepared in the native language for them to read and sign. If the solicitor is fluent in the foreign language then it is permissible for him/her to act in the role of the interpreter. However, this must be made clear either within the body of the statement or in a separate affidavit.

- A litigant in person should where possible use a certified interpreter when preparing a witness statement.

- If the witness cannot read or write in their own native language, the interpreter must carefully read the statement to the witness in his/her own language and set this out in the translator's jurat or affidavit, using the words provided by Annexes 1 or 2 to the Practice Direction. Once the statement has been completed and signed in the native language, it should be translated by a certified translator who should either then sign a jurat confirming the translation or provide a short affidavit confirming that she/he has faithfully translated the statement.

- If a witness is to give live evidence either in person or by video link a copy of the original statement in the witness's own language as well as in English should be provided for them well in advance of the hearing.

- If a statement has been obtained and prepared abroad in compliance with the country's laws a certified translation of that statement must be filed together with the original document.

Substance misuse

The Family Drug and Alcohol Court (FDAC)[66] provides a problem solving, therapeutic approach to care proceedings in cases where parental substance misuse is a key element. (See also Chapter 7 for cases where substance misuse is not an issue)

FDAC aims to improve outcomes for children by helping parents change the lifestyle that has negatively impacted on their parenting and put their children at risk of harm. The process tests whether parents can solve their problems and meet their children's needs in a timescale compatible with the children's needs, and make use of resources that can be accessed through the FDAC team or their partner agencies.

There are currently 13 FDAC teams working in 21 family courts covering 37 local authorities, with the FDAC teams funded by those local authorities. So, each local authority will be limited, by the extent of its funding, to a particular number of cases per year. The President of the Family Division speaking at the end of a Centre for Justice Innovation event in the House of Lords on 18 October 2023 backed the expansion of FDAC, telling ministers and parliamentarians that they should be in every court.

The difference between FDAC and non FDAC cases:

- Judicial continuity with specially trained judges allocated to these cases,

66 https://fdac.org.uk/introduction/

- An independent specialist, multi-disciplinary FDAC team linked to the court provides expert assessment and support to parents to effect and sustain change. Teams can include psychologists, psychiatrists, parental substance misuse specialist, primary mental health worker. This is distinct from the court directing ad hoc expert assessments, although FDAC can direct Part 25 expert assessments if the FDAC team does not have the appropriate expertise to give an opinion on a particular aspect of a case,

- Fortnightly court review meetings without lawyers where the allocated judge monitors progress, speaks directly to parents, FDAC team, the child's social worker and guardian, keeps parents engaged and motivated and explores ways of resolving problems. These review meetings are in addition to the usual lawyer – attended court hearings,

- A short updating report is filed with the court by the FDAC team and served on solicitors before the reviews,

- A record of the review is filed and served,

- No legal issues are discussed in reviews. If issues do arise e.g. regarding timetabling, this would result in the court listing the case for a further case management hearing at which lawyers would be present.

Advantages of FDAC:

- There is evidence that children are more likely to be re reunified or continued to live together with their primary carer compared to children with primary carers in non-FDAC care proceedings[67],

---

67 *Evaluation of Family Drug and Alcohol Courts Foundations – What Works Centre for Children & Families 2023*

- The perception FDAC is a more supportive process for parents, allowing them to demonstrate their ability to meet their child's needs, rather than feeling that the process is punitive,
- Extension to the 26-week court timetable can be made to allow work to be undertaken if there is positive progress,
- Parents individually assigned a key worker with whom they can develop a trusting relationship,
- Package of high-intensity, multidisciplinary support flexibly tailored for each individual following FDAC screening,
- Psychologists and psychiatrists undertake assessments working with the key worker,
- Opportunity to attend support groups e.g. The FDAC emotional regulation group, and the Circle of Security group which looks at attuned parenting,
- Dynamic assessment over time rather than a "snapshot",
- Assistance in securing long term support e.g. therapy,
- Judicial continuity with specially trained judges leading and providing active oversight to the whole case; having direct contact with parents, encouraging them to make and sustain changes,
- Some FDACs provide mentors, parents who have successfully completed the FDAC process and volunteer to support parents who are in proceedings,
- Some sites provide (pre-proceedings or) post proceedings support e.g. during a supervision order.

FDAC TIMELINE:

Week 0	local authority issues application
Week 1	First hearing for introduction and initial screening.
Week 2	Initial intervention planning meeting.
Week 3	FDAC initial assessment report and intervention plan submission.
Week 4	CMH sign up and trial for change officially begins.
Weeks 6, 8, 10, 12, 14 And 16	Fortnightly non-lawyer review hearings.
Week 10	Second intervention planning meeting.
Week 18	Third intervention planning meeting.
Week 19	FDAC review assessment.
Week 24	IRH and potential early final hearing within week 26, or potential contested final hearing.
Weeks 22–50	Potential further intervention planning meeting, minutes and review reports.
Weeks 34–50	Potential late final hearing.

Two recent first instances cases show why FDAC is so important.

Swindon Borough Council v B, C and Child A [2024] EWFC 8 (B) both parents were long term Class A drug users. The level of addiction was likely to require professional intervention and possible inpatient treatment. The mother achieved abstinence for three months and then relapsed. An application to adjourn the proceedings for a further period of time so that the mother could show she was committed to abstinence/reduction in taking drugs was refused. Care and Placement orders made.

In a postscript HHJ Caroline Wright raised serious concerns about the lack of support services offered to parents. The court raised that potentially there could have been a different outcome had the local authority agreed to use the FDAC model, which was available in the area.

In contrast, *Gloucestershire CC v A, B and C* [2024] EWFC 18 (B) both parents also had a long history of substance misuse. The mother's three older children could not remain in her care due to her drug use and involvement in abusive relationships. The parents achieved abstinence from drugs and benefited from a comprehensive package of support in respect of their substance misuse, mental health needs, the safety of their relationship with each other and their parenting of the child. The court made a final supervision order endorsing a supervision order support plan to ensure there was a "soft landing" after the FDAC process, where the child was supported to live with his parents by the same professionals who built up a relationship with them.

District Judge Tait concluded "*This is an example of why FDAC is so vital to the family justice system. It is built upon the ethos that no family wants their child to suffer and that every family in difficulty wants to make things better. People can change if they are offered the right support. Children belong with their parents if that can be safely achieved.*"

<u>Practice Points</u>

- Set expectations with clients about what FDAC entails including the extent of a lawyer's participation in FDAC.

- Request a copy of the protocol for the FDAC that your case is listed in.

- Be alive as to whether an expert outside of the FDAC multi-disciplinary team is necessary. Part 25 experts are rarely necessary in FDAC cases but there may be a specific question is outside of the FDAC team's areas of expertise.

- For non-lawyer reviews check your client has their FDAC report on their progress over the last two weeks.

- In cases of domestic abuse request separate non-lawyer reviews for a victim/survivor and perpetrator.

- Consider redaction of FDAC assessment reports before the report is shared with the other parent e.g. In cases of domestic abuse. Routine FDAC documents such as progress reviews or non-lawyer review minutes should not be shared with the other parent. If there is no agreement about redactions or non-service it should be referred to the FDAC judge to determine.

How does a case enter FDAC?

It is for the local authority to identify at the point of issuing care proceedings that a case may be suitable for FDAC. The decision should be taken in consultation with the professionals involved in the pre-proceedings process and in accordance with criteria agreed between the local authority and the FDAC team.

How can you help get a case into FDAC when it is for the local authority to select cases for FDAC?

- Check whether the local authority is part of an FDAC.

- Does the local authority still have availability to refer cases, or have they used up their annual quota of cases?

- If not, can the local authority "buy" a space in FDAC from another local authority?
- Has the local FDAC got availability to take the case?
- Is the type of case a referral that could be accepted by FDAC
- What is the waiting list?

Practice points

- Check whether there has been a discussion as part of the pre proceedings process with the professionals involved with the family as to whether the case is suitable for FDAC.
- What are the criteria between the local authority and the FDAC team?
- Make representations to the local authority to consider the case for FDAC.
- Ask the court for a direction that the local authority file and serve a statement setting out why they are not considering the case for FDAC or FDAC is not possible (if in an FDAC area). The local authority will include within a social worker's first statement a short assessment of why the case is suitable for FDAC but why not the other way round?
- Request the local authority put a package of support in place to replicate that which would be provided within FDAC, if the case is not in FDAC.

Assessing capacity

If the court is concerned that one of the parties in proceedings lacks the mental capacity to conduct proceedings, that issue must be addressed as a priority.

If a person lacks the mental capacity to conduct the proceedings they cannot conduct the litigation either as a litigant in person or through a solicitor. A litigation friend must be appointed for them *Family Procedure Rules r 15.2 and Practice Direction 15A.*

The C110A application asks the local authority if there are factors affecting litigation capacity.

Under the PLO *Family Procedure Rules 20210 Practice Direction 12A* the court gives standard directions on issue and allocation including appointing (if the person to be appointed consents) a litigation friend for any protected party (or any non-subject child who is a party) including the Official Solicitor where appropriate.

At the case management hearing the court is to give directions for the determination of any disputed issue about litigation capacity.

A person must be assumed to have capacity unless it is established that they lack capacity *Mental Capacity Act 2005 section 1(2).*

A person is not to be treated as unable to make a decision unless all practicable steps to help him to do so have been taken without success. *Mental Capacity Act 2005 section 1(3))*

A person is not to be treated as unable to make a decision merely because he makes an unwise decision. *Mental Capacity Act 2005 section 1(4)*.

> '*a person lacks capacity in relation to a matter if at the material time he is unable to make a decision for himself in relation to the matter because of an impairment of, or a disturbance in the*

functioning of, the mind or the brain" Mental Capacity Act 2005 section 2 (1)

The test can be broken down into three questions:

1) Is the person able to make a decision? If they cannot:

2) Is there an impairment or disturbance in the functioning of the person's mind or brain? If so:

3) Is the person's inability to make the decision because of the identified impairment or disturbance?

1) Is the person able to make a decision?

A person is unable to make a decision for himself if he is unable [68]

- to understand the information relevant to the decision,
- to retain that information,
- to use or weigh that information as part of the process of making the decision, or
- to communicate his decision (whether by talking, using sign language or any other means).

2) Is there an impairment or disturbance in the functioning of the person's mind or brain?

It is not necessary for the impairment or disturbance to fit into one of the diagnoses in the two main classification systems in psychiatry (ICD-11 or DSM-5)

68 Mental Capacity Act 2005 section 3(1)

It can include brain damage for example from a stroke, dementia, the symptoms of drug or alcohol abuse or conditions causing concussion, confusion or drowsiness. It can be temporary or permanent[69]

3) Is the person's inability to make the decision because of the identified impairment or disturbance?

There has to be a causal link between the disturbance or impairment and the inability to make the decision

Capacity is decision specific.[70]

Some people's ability to make decisions fluctuates because of the nature of their condition[71] and in those cases, it is particularly important to keep capacity under review throughout the proceedings.

The Family Justice Council have produced guidance *Capacity to Litigate in Proceedings involving Children*[72] which includes letters of instruction for treating or independent experts for capacity assessments.

The certificate of capacity to conduct proceedings to be completed by a medical professional can be found https://www.gov.uk/government/publications/certificate-as-to-capacity-to-conduct-proceedings

The Official Solicitor, the litigation friend of last resort, has produced a practice note about consenting to act in family case[73]:

---

69 Mental Capacity Act 2005 section 2(2)

70 *A Local Authority v JB* [2021] UKSC 52)

71 Family Procedure Rules 2020 Practice Direction 15B 4.1

72 https://www.judiciary.uk/wp-content/uploads/2018/04/capacity-to-litigate-in-proceedings-involving-children-april-2018.pdf

73 https://www.gov.uk/government/publications/appointment-of-official-solicitor-in-family-proceedings-practice-note

- if there nobody else is suitable and willing to be litigation friend
- there is money available to pay the Official Solicitor's costs, for example legal aid
- the person's doctor or another medical professional, confirms they lack capacity to manage the case (unless they are a child)

Practice Points

- Do not make assumptions and/or judgments.
- Tailor your approach to the individual parent. No two people will have the same communication profile
- Early identification and assessment of any additional needs a parent might have is essential.
- Consider with your client their strengths, challenges, triggers, communication preferences and what signs might there be of someone being outside their 'window of tolerance' with trauma responses.
- With your client you may want to prepare a one-page profile of them. This can travel with them throughout the proceedings, being provided to all professionals working with them including experts in the proceedings. It lets the parent be seen as a whole person, provides information about their communication profile, any adaptions they might need. The client does not have to keep repeating themselves and allows any professional working with the client to tailor their approach from the start of their working

relationship with the client. It is similar to person centred care planning[74]

- Learn more about your client's needs and any adjustments that might be possible. Think outside the standard adjustments. The Equal Treatment Bench Book contains a glossary at Appendix B of impairments and suggested adjustments. Communicourt have series of podcasts on different types of hidden disabilities and their impact on communication e.g. traumatic brain injury, stroke and bite size guides on conditions in their educational series The Access Brief series including communication tips.

- It is important to have focused expert assessments with appropriate experts with the requisite knowledge and experience tailored to the parent's needs. There are limitations in using standardised assessments tools for parents with additional needs.

- Ensure all meetings, including family group conferences (FGCs) take into account parental needs.

- Make sure there is partnership work with adult services e.g. updating or inviting adult services to meetings.[75]

- Check whether the social work team working with the parent are aware of the relevant guidance related to the parents needs and what recent training they have had.

- Consider lay advocacy support for your client including with the advocate participating in meetings.

74 https://www.england.nhs.uk/personalisedcare/pcsp/

75 *Re S* [2013] EWCA Civ 1073

- Review throughout the case that the local authority and courts are ensuring people with disabilities are not put at a substantial disadvantage contrary to *Equality Act 2010 section 20.*

- Try and ensure continuity with legal representatives, intermediaries, advocates, etc. who have an ongoing working relationship with the client, not just turn up on the day.

- Request that the local authority draft key documents e.g. threshold in a way that is accessible for the parents.[76]

- Consider what support is available including:

    - parent support services

    - in proceedings

    - emotional support

- Work together as a team for the parents with counsel, intermediaries, advocates, and any other support, all of whom have a different role to play.

- Consider referring to a community care solicitor if a Care Act assessment has not been undertaken for your client and work in partnership to ensure long term support is included for parents with a physical or mental impairment or illness.

- Have accessible information and communication for your clients with additional needs e.g. easy read (for example https://www.changepeople.org/ and

76 *Oxfordshire County Council v A mother (by her litigation friend, the Official Solicitor) and G* [2020] EWFC B40

https://www.photosymbols.com/) translated, with no legal jargon.

- Hold a directory of parent support services for parents with specific needs e.g. parenting groups, children's centres, parenting programmes, emotional support

- Request the judge give their judgment in a way that is accessible for parents.[77]

- Request that experts provide a short parent report specifically written (e.g. in 'easy read' English) and formatted in a way that is accessible for a parent

[77] *Z LBC v Mother* [2022] EWFC 63; *Local Authority v G (parents with a learning disability)* [2014] EWCA CIV 128 *Oxfordshire County Council v A mother (by her litigation friend, the Official Solicitor); G* [2020] EWFC B40; *Billie (A Child) (Care and Placement Orders)* [2024] EWFC 106(B)

CHAPTER FIVE

CASES WITH INTERNATIONAL ELEMENTS

International issues in care proceedings may arise in various ways including:

- Jurisdiction
- Relevant background information from agencies in other countries if a child and/or parents have lived outside of England and Wales, including court proceedings, police/criminal checks, children's services, and medical information from another jurisdiction
- Kinship placements outside of England and Wales including consideration of potential alternative carers, who can undertake any assessment, advice on mirror orders or recognition of orders under the 1996 Hague Convention
- Recognition in England and Wales of orders made in other countries
- Immigration issues including disclosure of documents between the family and immigration justice systems and, whether a child will have a right to remain in the country where their final care plan proposes they should be placed (whether that is in England and Wales or overseas)

Starting point

Under the PLO *Family Procedure Rules 2010 Practice Direction 12A* the local authority's application by form C110A should identify whether a case has any international aspects so the court can identify and consider any jurisdictional issues at the very start of proceedings. Form C110A should have attached relevant documents, including any foreign court orders and judgments/reasons and single, joint or inter-agency materials e.g. health and education/Home Office and Immigration Tribunal documents. These can assist in identifying any jurisdictional issues.

Within a day of issue (Day 2 of the timetable), the court must consider jurisdiction in a case with an international element. The standard directions on issue and allocation can include a requirement to identify whether a request has been made or should be made to a Central Authority or other competent authority in a foreign state or a consular authority in England and Wales in a case with an international element.

The court can consider a request from a party for an urgent preliminary CMH and where necessary can list a hearing and give additional directions.[1] This might include seeking disclosure of information from the Home Office via Form EX660 at this very early stage.[2] At the CMH the court will give detailed case management directions, including considering jurisdiction in a case with an international element. The parties' positions about jurisdiction should be available for the advocates meeting before the CMH.

Unless there is good reason (e.g. claims for asylum), the relevant foreign Embassy should be notified of proceedings if a party to proceedings is a foreign national.[3] Consulates have a role in offering support to their

1 Family Procedure Rules 2010 Practice Direction12A 2.4

2 *Re Y (Failure to Clarify Immigration Status)* [2024] EWFC 159

3 *International Family Justice Office: Family Courts Informing Consular Authorities of Proceedings*, and *Re E (A Child)* [2014] EWHC 6 (Fam).

citizens in the UK, which can mean having access to the child, where appropriate, or offering the child's family advice and support. A consular official might also ask to participate in or observe court proceedings.

Jurisdiction

The court must be satisfised by evidence that it has jurisdiction once all relevant parties have been able to adduce evidence on the issue. A court cannot determine that it has jurisdiction for proceedings by "default, concession or agreement". The standard form of order made at the first CMH includes the paragraph "*The court in England and Wales has jurisdiction in relation to the child[ren] on the basis that:...*" with the court's determination to be recorded there.

Jurisdiction in most cases will be governed by the *1996 Hague Convention on Jurisdiction, Applicable Law, Recognition, Enforcement and Co-operation in Respect of Parental Responsibility and Measures for the Protection of Children.*

After the UK left the European Union and the end of the transition period in 2020, Brussels IIa no longer applies to proceedings started after 1 January 2021.

Where the subject matter of an application falls outside the scope of the 1996 Convention, the rules under the *Family Law Act 1986* will have to be considered.

Whether there is a valid jurisdictional basis and what that basis is must be considered before or at the outset of proceedings, particularly where families have a clear connection to another country.[4]

4 *Re J (A Child) (1996 Hague Convention: Morocco)* [2015] EWCA Civ 329.

Jurisdiction under the 1996 Hague Convention

The 1996 Hague Convention governs jurisdiction in contracting states[5] in relation to measures directed to the person or property of the child (*Article 1(a) 1996 Hague Convention on Jurisdiction, Applicable Law, Recognition, Enforcement and Co-operation in Respect of Parental Responsibility and Measures for the Protection of Children*).

Chapter II sets out the jurisdictional scheme applying to care proceedings. This includes measures about the exercise, termination and restriction of parental responsibility as well as delegation, and the placement of a child in a foster family or institutional care (*Article 15 – 22 1996).*

Jurisdiction to take measures directed to protect the child's person or property lies with the courts of the member state where the child is habitually resident (*Article 5*). The 1996 Convention provides no definition of habitual residence.

The Practical Handbook on the Operation of the 1996 Child Protection Convention suggests that there may be different considerations to take into account when determining habitual residence for the purposes of the 1996 Convention. The handbook[6] refers to habitual residence being a "factual concept".

Under Brussels II the test for habitual residence was also factual and case law has given us assistance:

- It follows from the ordinary use of the words that residence must have "*a certain permanence or regularity*" (*Mercredi v Chaffe* (Case C-497/10) [2011] 1 FLR 1293).

5 https://www.hcch.net/en/states/hcch-members

6 The *Practical Handbook on the Operation of the 1996 Child Protection Convention* Chapter 4 paragraph 4.4

- Habitual residence does not require "*the child's full integration in the environment of the new state, but only a degree of it*". (*Re B (A Child)* [2016] UKSC 4).

- It is "*the place which reflects some degree of integration by the child in a social and family environment*" (*A v A (Children: Habitual Residence)* [2013] UKSC 60).

- What is significant is not the permanence of the residence but its stability. "*there is therefore no requirement that a child be resident in the country for any particular period and no requirement on the part of one or both parents to reside in that country indefinitely or permanently* "(*Re R (Children) Reunite International Child Abduction Centre intervening* [2016] AC 76).

- "*The relevant reality is that of the child, not the parents* "(*Re LC (Children)* [2014] UKCS 1).

- MacDonald, J provided a non-exhaustive list of factors when considering habitual residence in *E v D* [2022] EWHC 1216 (Fam).

- *"Some degree of integration' is not itself determinative of the question of habitual residence. Habitual residence is an issue of fact which requires consideration of all relevant factors There is an open ended, not a closed, list of potentially relevant factors""_Re A (Habitual Residence: 1996 Hague Child Protection Convention)* [2023] EWCA Civ 659.

When should habitual residence be determined?

Article 5 does not specify when the child's habitual residence is to be determined, whether at the date of the application or the date of the trial.

The decision in *LB of Hackney v P & Ors* [2023] EWCA Civ 1213 determined the relevant date for establishing jurisdiction under *Article 5*, an issue that had troubled the High Court since the UK left the EU. The date should initially be determined by reference to the date on which proceedings were commenced.

Lord Justice Moylan's conclusions on the issue of jurisdiction were:

(i) the 1996 Convention applies to proceedings for an order under Part IV of the Children Act 1989;

(ii) the court must determine the issue of jurisdiction at the outset of proceedings by reference to the date on which the proceedings were commenced;

(iii) jurisdiction under the 1996 Convention can be lost during the course of proceedings, if it was based on habitual residence and the child has ceased to be habitually resident in England and Wales. Accordingly, the court must be satisfied that it retains jurisdiction at the final hearing;

(iv) jurisdiction is acquired under *Article 5* from the date on which a child becomes habitually resident in England and Wales; the effect of this on existing proceedings will depend on the circumstances of the case;

(v) the court in England and Wales will likely have jurisdiction to make interim orders under Part IV under *Article 11* when the child is habitually resident in a Contracting State;

(vi) the court in England and Wales will likely have jurisdiction to make interim orders under Part IV under *Article 11* and will also have substantive jurisdiction based on a child's presence here when the child is habitually resident in a non-Contracting State.

When habitual residence cannot be determined

Cases in which a child's habitual residence cannot be established will be exceptional.[7]

For refugee children and children who, due to disturbances occurring in their country, are internationally displaced, the authorities of the state where the children are present have jurisdiction (*Article 6*).

Presence in this country but habitually resident in another country

Y&E (1996 Hague Convention: Article 11) [2023] EWCA Civ 817 Lord Justice Baker gave the judgment of the Court of Appeal in a successful appeal against the first instance judge's decision to conclude care proceedings. The case involved a family living in Spain who are British and have property and family in this jurisdiction. The mother and children lived in Spain whilst the father remained in England for work, travelling to Spain frequently to visit them. During a holiday in England, whilst staying at the family home that was in the process of being sold, the younger child was presented to hospital with a stab wound that required surgery.

In respect of a child present in this country but habitually resident in another country that is a signatory to the Convention:

- The court of the other country has primary jurisdiction to take child protection measures under *Article 5*;

- The English family court has the power to take urgent measures under *Article 11* or provisional measures under *Article 12* in respect of the children, which may take the form of interim care

7 *Re L (A Child)* [2012] EWCA Civ 1157

orders under *section 38 Children Act 1989* modified by Reg 5 of the Regulations.

- Those urgent or provisional measures shall lapse as soon as the authorities which have jurisdiction under *Articles 5* to *10* have taken a decision in respect of the measures of protection which may be required by the situation;

- If the English court considers it is better placed to assess the child's best interests, it may submit a request under *Article 9* that it be authorised to exercise jurisdiction to take the measures of protection which it considers to be necessary.

Baker LJ expressed his provisional view that consistent with Charles, J in *Re S (Care: Jurisdiction)* [2008] EWHA 3013 (Fam) *"Any interim measures relying on article 20 (or in other cases where a return to another country so that it will make the future decisions is necessary or contemplated) are by definition interim. What will be required, and properly regarded as interim, will be case and fact sensitive and will be informed by co-operation and liaison…It will be unusual for this court under article 20 (or in other such cases) to embark on fact-finding hearings…"* that a similar approach should now apply to *Article 11* of the Convention. In this case the court should have obtained the actual or likely response of the Spanish authorities to the *Article 9* request prior to conducting a fact-finding hearing.

Re A & Ors (Case Proceedings: 1996 Hague Convention: Habitual Residence) [2024] EWFC 110 provides a useful example of the court determining jurisdiction and analysing practice and procedure in public law cases which originate in the international movement of children. Knowles, J highlighted the need for more detailed guidance on public law cases which originate in the international movement of children, whether or not these are associated with a claim for asylum.

The court noted the following on habitual residence:

- The essential question was whether the children had achieved a sufficient degree of integration into a social and family environment in England.

- The court's focus must be on present circumstances, but an understanding of the children's past experiences fed into a holistic analysis of their current situation.

- Though their status in this jurisdiction was uncertain, this factor did not of itself operate to prevent the children becoming habitually resident. Thus, looking at the children's present situation, it demonstrated the necessary degree of stability and sufficient integration into a social and family environment to be described as habitual.

Having decided that the children were habitually resident in England, the judge was provisionally of the view that immigration and asylum law did not prevent her making interim care orders.

Jurisdiction under Family Law Act 1986

The Family Law Act 1986 applies to issues of jurisdiction where the 1996 Hague Convention is not applicable.

It applies to:

- An order under section 8 Children Act 1989 Family Law Act 1986 section 1(1)(a)

- A special guardianship orders Family Law Act 1986 section 1(1)(aa)

- Orders for contact under section 26 of the Adoption and Children Act 2002 Family Law Act 1986 section 1(1) (ab)

- an order for post adoption contact under section 51A of the Adoption and Children Act 2002 Family Law Act 1986 section 1((1) (ac)

- Orders made under the inherent jurisdiction of the High Court that give the care of the child to any person; provide for contact; or make provision for the child's education Family Law Act 1986 section 1 (1)(d).

Inherent jurisdiction

Family Law Act 1986 section 2(3) provides for certain orders to be made under the inherent jurisdiction of the court. These include orders that:

- Give the care of the child to any person.

- Provide for contact.

- Make provisions for the child's education.

These orders can be made where:

- Family Law Act 1986 section 2(3)(a) the court has jurisdiction under the 96 Hague Convention; or

- Family Law Act 1986 section 2 (3)(b)(ii) – if the 1996 Hague Convention does not apply, but:

    - the child is habitually resident or is present in England and Wales and not habitually resident in any part of the UK or

    - The child is present in England and Wales on the relevant date and the court considers that the immediate exercise of its power is necessary for the child's protection

Information

Communication with authorities in the overseas country is vital to ascertain how best to obtain relevant information and records.[8]

Assessments

Identifying the right person to undertake the assessment of a person overseas is crucial. There are advantages and disadvantages to each option. There may be gaps in the assessment whichever option is chosen. Regarding the issue of who undertakes an assessment, and how, the court needs actively to consider the legality and necessity of the assessment type.

Options

- Through the Central Authority

  Likely to be of interest to the local authority as there is no charge to obtain an assessment through a Central Authority.

- Via Children and Families Across Borders (CFAB) to obtain a local assessment

  If a local assessment is being undertaken foreign authorities need to have all necessary information and for it to be carefully documented what has been sent to them.[9]

- Social worker/ISW travelling

  Guidance has discouraged social workers from England and Wales travelling overseas to conduct assessment. It may be illegal

8 *Re K, T and U (Placement of Children with Kinship Carers Abroad)* [2019] EWFC 59

9 *Re V-Z(Children)* [2016] EWCA Civ 475

in some countries (under local law and rules governing the practice of social work) as well as presenting ethical challenges.[10]

The CFAB factsheet *UK Social Worker's Conducting Assessments Overseas* includes a checklist of key questions to consider if a social worker from England and Wales is considering travelling abroad to carry out an overseas assessment.

Enquiries would need to be undertaken *before* a social worker travelled outside this jurisdiction to undertake an assessment.[11] This will also include viability assessments and online assessments.[12]

Re KM (A Child) (Welfare) [2023] EWFC 313 is an example of a case where an English ISW travelled overseas to a non-Hague Convention contracting state to undertake an assessment, in that case of the parents. The visit was facilitated by officials in the overseas country with significant assistance from the Embassy of that country in England.

- Collaborative assessment between the visiting social worker working alongside a local social worker

  CFAB considers this to be best practice.[13]

---

10 https://www.ifsw.org/policy-and-guiding-principles-for-international-social-work-assessment-of-children/#:~:text=It%20is%20likely%20to%20be,consequently%20producing%20a%20misleading%20assessment; *UK Social Worker's Conducting Assessments Overseas factsheet, CFAB*)

11 *Leicester City Council v S & Ors* [2014] EWHC 1575(Fam)

12 *Re V-Z (Children)* [2016] EWCA Civ 475

13 *UK Social Worker's Conducting Assessments Overseas factsheet, CFAB*

- Consider inviting the proposed carer to the UK for the assessment

Placements

There is an implied duty on local authorities to explore the wider family, either to support the parents and child or to identify them as potential carers.[14]

Alternative potential carers should be identified at an early stage so that assessments can be considered and started promptly.

Requests for information about a potential carer:

- Are made through the International Child Abduction and Contact Unit (ICACU) for English cases and the Welsh Government for Welsh cases if the country is a 1996 Hague Convention contracting state,

- Thought should be given to who to approach for assistance e.g. CFAB, or consular services if the potential carer lives in a non-Hague Convention contracting state.

Where the proposed carers appear to be viable, the assessment of carers living in another country could justify an extension of 26 weeks' time limit for care proceedings because of the time needed for an assessment to be carried out and there may unavoidable delays.[15]

---

14 *Re H (Care and Adoption: Assessment of wider family)* [2019] EWFC 10

15 *Family Justice Council: interim guidance on special guardianship, Public Law Working Group, Recommendations to achieve best practice in the child protection and family justice system 2020*

It is important to provide proposed carers living abroad with legal advice (funded by the local authority) on the proposed orders and support packages as with any alternative carers.

Other jurisdictions may not be familiar with the types of orders in England and Wales e.g. special guardianship orders. International adoption is a more difficult route to follow than proceedings under a special guardianship order. This is because other jurisdictions' approaches to adoption can be fundamentally different to that taken in England and Wales, e.g. it might be an option only if there is no possibility that a child could return to their parents' care (for instance if their parents are deceased).

Advice may be needed on:

- The effect of any order made in England and Wales in the overseas jurisdiction.
- Whether any order would be recognised (especially where the overseas jurisdiction is a non-1996 Hague Convention contracting state).
- Are mirror orders needed? It may not be possible for courts in a non-1996 Hague Convention contracting state to make an order which mirrors exactly the terms of a UK order. Is it possible to obtain a mirror order before the child moves overseas?
- Suggested wording of any order.
- What family orders may be required in the other jurisdiction to ensure the children and carers are safe, and/or are able to secure education, financial support, housing etc.
- Whether the foreign authorities will need to approve the placement of the child in their jurisdiction.

- Is there a need for other assessments to be undertaken in the overseas jurisdiction?

- What documents will need to be provided to the carers, and do they need to be translated, legalised/apostilled, authenticated etc.?

Advice on foreign orders

The court may need expert evidence on foreign law to determine issues such as the effect of any existing foreign orders, who has parental responsibility and assisting with who is an automatic respondent to proceedings[16] or any issues of dispensing with service.[17]

Immigration issues

The President of the Family Division and the Home Office have agreed a Protocol *Communicating with UK Visas and Immigration (UKVI) in Family Proceedings*[18] to obtain immigration and visa information for use in family court proceedings i.e.:

- Form EX660 must be completed by the parties and approved by the judge,

- An approved and sealed order provided,

- The UKVI SVEC pro-forma completed by the court staff.

---

16 Family Procedure Rules 2020 r12.3

17 Family Procedure Rules rule r.6.36

18 https://www.judiciary.uk/guidance-and-resources/protocol-communicating-with-uk-visas-and-immigration-ukvi-in-family-proceedings/

Requesting disclosure from the Home Office via Form EX660 of information on the immigration status of the child and the parents should be an initial step. The Home Office are committed to responding within four weeks, although in practice replies tend to take much longer than this, adding to the need for the request for information to be made as soon as possible.

In *Re Y (Failure to Clarify Immigration Status)* [2024] EWFC 159 Mr Justice MacDonald set out that directions should be given at the CMH for securing the evidence or expert opinion required to address any issues at the IRH, or at the final hearing if one is required, *before* a final order is made. It was not acceptable for issues regarding immigration status to be left to be investigated at the IRH or final hearing and even less acceptable for them to be left unresolved at the point the court makes a final order.

In *Re Y*, the child had been subject to care proceedings which concluded with a special guardianship order in the maternal aunt's favour. At the point of the final order being made the child had no immigration status in the United Kingdom and faced difficulties securing immigration status in Turkey. The court appeared to have proceeded on the basis that further steps would be taken with respect to regularising the child's immigration status in this country, with the assistance of the local authority, without any clarity as to what those steps were or the chances that they would be successful.

The special guardian applied back to court eighteen months later for recitals requesting that the Secretary of State for the Home Department grant the child British Citizenship or a recital summarising the intention of the court at the conclusion of the care proceedings. The application was refused as an impermissible attempt to influence the Secretary of State by obtaining an expression of opinion from the court on matters which are for the Secretary of State to decide, although permission was given to disclose specific documents from the care proceedings to the to the Secretary of State for the Home Department.

Careful consideration should be given to disclosure of parents and children's immigration documents into proceedings. Asylum applications made pursuant to the *1951 Convention Relating to the Status of Refugees* are confidential at common law, and pursuant to international law and practice guidance[19].

Immigration advice might be needed in England and Wales.

For a placement overseas advice will be needed on:

- the immigration status of the children in the other jurisdiction
- what steps will need to be taken to ensure the children can live permanently in the other jurisdiction
- what visa and other travel documents may be required for the children to enter the other jurisdiction

Funding experts in cases with international issues

The costs of and expenses relating to ISWs is not an allowable disbursement where such work is provided outside England and Wales.[20] The local authority will need to be invited to pay for any assessment.

Where the court requires advice on foreign law to enable them to make an order in England and Wales that is in scope for legal aid.[21] However, if once the order was made in the UK and the client wanted to obtain mirror orders overseas, this would be out of scope.[22]

---

19 *Re H* [2020] EWCA Civ 1001

20 *Guidance on Renumeration of Expert Witnesses paragraph 7.180*

21 *Legal Aid Sentencing and Punishment of Offenders Act 2012 section 32*

22 Guidance on Renumeration of Expert Witnesses paragraph 5.37

Expert advice on immigration law in a foreign jurisdiction can be provided by[23]:

- A legal practitioner who is qualified to practice in England and Wales who has verifiable expertise in the immigration law of the country concerned:
    - A solicitor's firm would be paid by way of standard hourly rates[24];
    - Counsel would be paid by way of standard hourly rates[25], or
- A legal practitioner not qualified to practice in England and Wales but in another jurisdiction who is a Court ordered expert in the immigration law of the country concerned would be paid as an expert. As there are no codified rates you need to apply for prior authority. The Legal Aid Agency would then use its discretion[26] to determine the most appropriate rate to pay, or
- An individual who is not a legal practitioner but who is a Court ordered expert in the immigration law of the country concerned would be paid as an expert. As there are no codified rates you need to apply for prior authority. The Legal Aid Agency would then use its discretion.

---

23 Guidance on Renumeration of Expert Witnesses paragraph 5.40

24 Civil Legal Aid (Renumeration) Regulations 2013 Schedule 1, table 10(b)

25 Civil Legal Aid (Renumeration) Regulations 2013 Schedule 2

26 Civil Legal Aid (Renumeration) Regulations 2013 Schedule 5, paragraph 3

Practice Points

- Although on issue of proceedings the court's focus is on jurisdiction, give early consideration to the other international issues that may need to be addressed e.g. gathering information from overseas agencies.

- Very early consideration is needed with the client of their and the child's immigration status, (dual) nationality, where has a child lived previously, how long have they been in England and Wales, and connections overseas to put together information necessary for the court to determine jurisdiction. Take copies of children's and parents' identification, travel and immigration documents. It is important to recognise that the immigration status of parents and children may not be the same.

- Clarify with the client whether there is any reason they would have concerns if relevant consular officials were contacted.

- Identify potential carers overseas, gathering contact details, and consideration of their assessment.

- Communicate with CFAB who can offer support with social work and law and have external connections with agencies:

    - free Advice Line, five days a week, to provide guidance and practical support on international kinship care cases and overseas placements

    - Legal Advice Services offer legal support with cross-border children's cases, including expert reports from legal partners overseas.

- Consider the advantages and disadvantages of each type of assessment.

- Orders for disclosure will be required for documentation from the family proceedings to be disclosed to any immigration solicitors making applications on your client's behalf and the relevant immigration authorities.

- Identify lawyers in other jurisdictions who could provide advice on the recognition of orders made in England and Wales. For example via International Academy of Family Lawyers (https://www.iafl.com/find-a-lawyer/) or Careful Child Relocation (https://carefulchildrelocation.com/find-a-lawyer-or-mediator/).

- Any letters of instruction to experts based out of the jurisdiction should be clear, jargon free and explain legal concepts in this jurisdiction where necessary.

CHAPTER SIX

FINAL ORDERS

There are two stages in care proceedings, the threshold stage, and the welfare stage.

The local authority has to satisfy the court that the threshold criteria are met, on the balance of probabilities and in accordance with the Children Act 1989 section 31(2). See Chapter 1 for discussion.

The court may, in certain limited circumstances, decide to conduct a 'split' hearing, to consider threshold separately from deciding on welfare, for instance in cases of alleged inflicted injury (specifically if there are no other concerns about the child's welfare, and/or if the court needs to make findings of fact before professionals and experts can make welfare recommendations). However, more usually the court will decide threshold and welfare at the same time.

At the welfare stage of proceedings, a court considers the outcome which will meet the child's best interests *Children Act 1989 s 1 (1).*

A finding that the threshold criteria are satisfied does not automatically lead to the making of a care order (or a supervision order). It is, rather, the gateway that opens up the possibility of orders being made.

In making the welfare decision, the court must take account of the *section 1(3) Children Act 1989 welfare checklist* and ,if the local authority plan is adoption, and there is an application for a placement order, the *section 1(4) Adoption and Children Act 2002* welfare checklist. The court must then have regard to the realistic options put forward, taking a holistic and balanced as opposed to linear approach, consistent with the guidance given in *Re B-S (Children)* [2013] EWCA Civ 1146.

To achieve this, the court is required to conduct a side-by-side analysis of the pros and cons of each realistic placement option. *"a balancing exercise in which each option is evaluated to the degree of detail necessary to analyse and weigh its own internal positives and negatives and each option is then compared, side by side, against the competing option or option"* *G (A Child)* [2013] EWCA Civ 965, cited and approved in *Re H-W (children)* [2022] 4 All ER 683.

In reaching a final decision the court must start from the position that the least interventionist alternative is to be preferred applying *section 1(5) Children Act 1989* and *section 1(6) of the Adoption and Children Act.* The court must not make an order unless they consider that doing so would be better for the child than making no order *section 1(5) Children Act 1989.*

The court must have regard to and balance the Article 8 ECHR rights of the child and each parent to respect for private and family life. Where there is a tension between the parents' and the child's Article 8 rights, it is the child's right that prevails.[1] Each case must be determined on its own facts in accordance with the proportionate approach pursuant to *Re B (Care: Interference with Family Life)* [2003] 2 FLR 813. The court must not make a care order unless it is satisfied it is both necessary and proportionate and no other less radical form of order would achieve the need to promote the welfare of the child.

Wherever possible, consistent with their welfare needs, children deserve an upbringing within their natural families. Care plans for adoption are made when "*necessary*" for the protection of the children's interests, which means "*when nothing else will do*", "*when all else fails.*" *Adoption "should only be contemplated as a last resort"* *Re B* [2013] UKSC 33; *Re P* (a child) [2013] EWCA Civ 963; *Re G* (a child) [2013] EWCA Civ 965.

1 *Yousef v The Netherlands* [2003] 1 FLR 210

"*Nothing else will do* "is not a substitute for a proper welfare evaluation.[2] *In the Matter Of M (A Child)* [2024] EWCA Civ 1000 the Court of Appeal considered the holistic exercise required in considering adoption as a placement option, the need for adequate reasons and analysis in any judgment, and the importance of the judge keeping an open mind until he/she has been able to evaluate the evidence and formulate his/her reasons and analysis

Care orders at home

For the first time since *Re D (Child Under Care Order: Injunction under Human Rights Act 1998)* [2014] EWFC 6, the Court of Appeal considered in *JW (Child at Home Under Care Order)* [2023] EWCA Civ 944 the approach to be taken when proceedings conclude with a plan for a child to be placed, or remain living, at home with a parent. Specifically, the court looked at whether a final care order, supervision order or no order should be made. In the leading judgment the President of the Family Division noted there had been regional variations in the approach taken.

The case provides a summary of the statutory framework and case law:

- Making a care order with a subject child placed at home in the care of their parents is permissible within the statutory scheme and express provision is made in *Children Act 1989, section 22C* and in the placement regulations;

- The High Court decision in *Re DE (Child under Care Order: Injunction under Human Rights Act 1998)* ([2014] EWFC 6) containing guidance endorsed by the President, has been widely accepted. That decision states that, in all but a true emergency, the local authority power to remove a child from their home

2 *Re W (Adoption: Approach to Long-Term Welfare)* [2016] EWCA Civ 793

under an existing care order should not be exercised without giving parents an opportunity to bring the issue before a court;

- The difference in removing a child from home when there is an existing care order, as opposed to there being an application for a care order with a plan of removal, is now largely procedural. In all but the most urgent cases, removal (when there is already a care order) will ultimately be decided by the court, not by a local authority acting administratively;

- A care order means that the local authority shares parental responsibility with parents, which is important, but the fact that considerable help and advice may be needed over a prolonged period is not a reason, in itself, for making a care order;

- It is wrong to make a care order in order to impose duties on a local authority or use it to encourage them to perform the duties that they have to a child in need;

- The protection of the child is the decisive factor, but proportionality is key when making the choice between a care and supervision order for a child who is placed at home;

- Supervision orders should be made to work, where that is the proportionate form of order to make.

The President endorsed the recommendations and best practice guidance in the Public Law Working Group's report *Recommendations to achieve best practice in the child protection and family justice systems* [3] which expressly dealt with the making of care orders where children are placed at home (paragraphs 158 to 162). The President summarised five important principles:

---

3 https://www.judiciary.uk/wp-content/uploads/2021/03/March-2021-report-final_clickable.pdf

- A care order should not be used solely as a vehicle to achieve the provision of support and services after the conclusion of proceedings;

- A care order on the basis that the child will be living at home should only be made when there are exceptional reasons for doing so. It should be rare in the extreme that the risks of significant harm to a child are judged to be sufficient to merit the making of a care order but, nevertheless, the risks can be managed with the child remaining in the care of parents;

- Unless, in an exceptional case, a care order is necessary for the protection of the child, some other means of providing support and services must be used;

- Where a child is to be placed at home, the making of a supervision order to support reunification may be proportionate;

- Where a supervision order is being considered, the best practice guidance in the Public Law Working Group April 2023 report must be applied. In particular the court should require the local authority to have a supervision support plan in place.

Supervision orders

A supervision order can contain requirements as follows:

- A requirement for the supervised child to comply with the directions of the supervisor on certain specific matters *Children Act 1989, Sch 3, para 2 (1).*

- With the consent of any person with parental responsibility for the child and with whom the child lives ('the responsible person'[1]) a requirement for the responsible person to take certain steps or to comply with the supervisor's directions *Children Act 1989, Sch 3, para 3(1).*

- A requirement that the supervised child submits to specified medical or psychiatric examination (*Children Act 1989, Sch 3,para 4(1)*).

- Provided certain conditions are satisfied, a requirement that the supervised child shall submit for such treatment concerning his mental health as may be specified (*Children Act 1989, Sch 3, para 5(1)).*

These conditions are rarely used as they are not enforceable. However, breaches may be relied on as evidence in any further proceedings.

A further Public Law Working Group report has been published *Recommendations to achieve best practice in the child protection and family justice systems: Supervision Orders.*[4] There is an expectation that, in every case where a supervision order may be made, the local authority will prepare a clear and detailed supervision support plan which is tailored to the needs of the child.[5] The plan should be clear as to the provision of resources to underpin each element of the plan, and that the plan should be seen as a living instrument and be kept under formal 'robust' review during the life of the supervision order.

4 https://www.judiciary.uk/wp-content/uploads/2023/04/April-2023-Report-Supervision-Orders-Final.pdf

5 https://www.judiciary.uk/wp-content/uploads/2023/04/Annex-A-Supervision-Order-Plan.pdf

Section 20 Children Act 1989

The President's Public Law Working Group's *Best practice guidance: Section 20 / section 76 accommodation*[6] makes it clear that section 20 agreements can, in appropriate cases, be used to underpin longer term placements. The guidance sets out best practice on section 20 agreements.

The parameters of section 20 can be summarised as follows:

- Parents may ask the local authority to accommodate a child as part of the services they provide for children in need *Williams & Another v London Borough of Hackney* [2018] UKSC 37.

- A local authority cannot provide accommodation if any person who has parental responsibility and is able to provide or arrange for accommodation to be provided for the child objects *(Children Act 1989*).

- There is no statutory limit on the duration of the provision of accommodation made under section 20 as confirmed in *Williams v London Borough of Hackney.*

- Whilst a person with parental responsibility may not surrender or transfer any part of their parental responsibility, they may delegate it by arranging for some or all of it to be met by one or more persons on their behalf (*Children Act 1989 section 2(9)*). In agreeing to accommodation a parent is '*simply delegating the exercise of her parental responsibility for the time being to the local authority*': *Williams v London Borough of Hackney.*

6 https://www.judiciary.uk/wp-content/uploads/2021/03/S-20-s-76-BPG-report_clickable.pdf

- Any person with parental responsibility may at any time remove the child from the accommodation (*Children Act 1989 section 20 (8)*)

- If there is a child arrangements order naming a person with whom the child is to live and that person agrees to the child being accommodated, then no other person with parental responsibility may either object to the placement under *section 20 (7)* or remove the child from the accommodation under *section 20(8).*

  (*Re S and Re W* [2020] EWCA Civ 1)

The Court of Appeal considered the interplay between section 20 and section 31 Children Act 1989 in *Re S and Re W* [2020] EWCA Civ 1. These were two cases of children who were settled in long-term placements which were meeting their respective needs, and both the placements and the accompanying care plans were supported by the parents. It was held that – in that case – the granting a care order was not a proportionate response to an unsubstantiated risk that the child's father might disrupt the placement and remove the child from the section 20 accommodation.

No order

Is there a sufficiently detailed plan to support a return home? In some areas, a 'child in need' plan may be used as part of a support plan. In other areas, the local authority might convene a child protection conference in order to formulate a child protection plan. In either case, the plan needs to be in place before the proceedings end.

Long term foster care v adoption

The Court of Appeal has given guidance about the different considerations that apply to long-term fostering and adoption in *V (Children)* [2013] EWCA Civ 913:

- Adoption makes the child a permanent part of the adoptive family to which he or she fully belongs;

- If a child is fostered, the parents may apply for the discharge of a care order with a view to the child returning to their care. In contrast, once an adoption order is made, it is made for all time;

- Contact within adoption is also a different matter from contact with a child in care;

- Routine life is different for the adopted child in that once he or she is adopted, the local authority has no further role in his or her life (no local authority medicals, no local authority reviews, no need to consult the social worker over school trips abroad, for example).

When faced with a choice between adoption and fostering, the court's primary task is to take a decision as to whether one or the other is right for the child as a matter of principle. In order to do that, it will not usually be necessary to have evidence about the availability of placements: *Re T (Placement Order)* (CA) [2008] EWCA Civ 248.

Joe (a child) (Long term foster care versus adoption) [2023] EWFC 174 is a first instance decision in which the court refused to make a placement order and rejected the local authority's care plan of adoption. The court found that long term foster care would provide a stable placement and offered permanence for the child who was aged four.

The judge made reference to the main conclusion in the Care Enquiry 2013.[7] *"From all that we have learnt – is that 'permanence' for children means 'security, stability, love and a strong sense of identity and belonging'. This is not connected to legal status, and one route to . . . permanency is not*

---

7 https://www.nuffieldfoundation.org/sites/default/files/files/Care%20Inquiry%20-%20Full%20Report%20April%202013.pdf)

necessarily better than . . . another: each option is . . . right . . . for some children and young people. Adoption, although right for some children, will only ever provide permanence for a small number of children in care."

This case is at first instance and so is persuasive at most and is of course fact specific with the court finding that Joe was strongly and positively attached to his foster carer, who was committed to caring for him till he was 18, and beyond. Interestingly, the judge addressed some of the generalisations that are often put forward argued when she was scrutinising the options for this child and largely rejected them as applying in this case. The judge rejected arguments that:

- Long term fostering is not a permanent option. The judge noted that long term fostering is a legally defined permanence option for looked after children.[8]

- Long term fostering will deny a child a sense of security from a young age and will not allow him to grow up feeling secure in a family placement. In this case, Joe was secure in his placement.

- Growing up as a looked after child will place a burden on the child that may affect his attachments and sense of security. The judge commented that an adopted child can also feel stigmatised.

- The fact that the foster carer will not commit to a placement that is legally permanent is of concern. This was rejected by the judge, who relied on evidence from the foster carer of her long-term commitment to Joe.

---

8 Care Planning and Fostering Miscellaneous Amendments England Regulations 2015. The related statutory guidance has been incorporated into a revision of *The Children Act 1989 Guidance and Regulations Volume 2: Care Planning, Placement and Case Review*

- The level of intrusion by the local authority under a care order would not be in the child's best interest. The level of intrusion could be reduced over time by the local authority delegating day to day decision making to the foster carer.

- The child will lose the chance of a forever family. In this case, the foster carer was offering a commitment to care for Joe till he was 18, and there was no reason to think she – or Joe – would then no longer think of him as part of the family.

In *Re D- S (A Child: Adoption or fostering)* [2024] EWCA Civ 948 the Court of Appeal considered a first instance decision refusing a placement order in respect of a child of eleven months on the basis that it had not been established that "*nothing else would do.*". The court determined that the judge had fallen into the error of using "*nothing else would do*" as a substitute for a proper welfare evaluation, whereas it applies only as a "proportionality cross-check".

The case reviews the law and case law regarding long-term fostering and adoption.

Special Guardianship orders

The Public Law Working Group report *Recommendations to achieve best practice in the child protection and family justice systems: Special guardianship orders Special guardianship orders*[9] was produced following the decision in *P-S (Children)* [2018] EWCA Civ 1407. It includes suggestions for best practice:

- The need in every case for a 'robust and comprehensive' special guardianship assessment and support plan.

9 https://www.judiciary.uk/wp-content/uploads/2021/03/Special-guardianship-BPG-report_Clickable.pdf

- An emphasis on parental contact and the need to consider what professional input may be required to support contact in the future.

In Re S (Adoption Order or Special Guardianship Order) [2007] EWCA Civ 54 the Court of Appeal endorsed a schedule of the main differences between special guardianship orders and adoption orders which was included as an annex to the Court of Appeal judgment in *Re AJ (Adoption Order or Special Guardianship Order)* [2007] EWCA Civ 55.

Re S also gave illustrations of some of the circumstances in which special guardianship might be appropriate:

- Older children who do not wish to be legally separated from their birth family.

- Children being cared for on a permanent basis by members of their wider birth family.

- Children in some minority ethnic communities, who have religious and cultural difficulties with adoption.

- Unaccompanied asylum-seeking children who need secure permanent homes but have strong attachments to their family abroad.

Practice Points

If a child is to remain at or return home with your client:

- Where a child remains or returns home, scrutinise support plans.

- Ensure any support plan is clear and tailored.

- Request clarification and asked for it to be evidenced in the plan, that each element of support is resourced and funded.
- How frequently will the plan be reviewed?
- Consider whether a family group conference should be arranged before the conclusion of proceedings, to consider who, within the family network, can commit to offering support (and what, specifically, they are offering to do).
- If discussions about the plans take place at a final hearing, seek a direction for an amended plan to be filed.
- Consider whether a section 17 assessment should be requested, to confirm the range and level of services that the local authority could provide under section 17 to meet the child's needs.

CHAPTER SEVEN

CONTACT

Contact with a child in care

Research *Contact following placement in care, adoption, or special guardianship: implications for children and young people's wellbeing* Nuffield Family Justice Observatory July 2020 [1] shows us just how crucial decisions about contact are for children, whatever their placement. It is important to understand the purpose of contact. It may be intended to support children's return home, help them to maintain or build relationships with family members, help them to manage loss and separation, or to make sense of the past as part of life story and identity work. The key messages from the Nuffield Family Observatory report are:

- Focus on the quality of contact.
- Listen to the views of children and young people.
- Recognise the significance of siblings, grandparents, wider family and friends. There is still too often a narrow view of 'family'.
- Ensure that everyone involved is clear about the purpose of contact, which will vary depending on the circumstances of the child and the long-term plans for the child's future.

---

1 https://www.nuffieldfjo.org.uk/resource/contact-well-being; Contact between children in care or adopted and their families: six key messages from research – Nuffield Family Justice Observatory (nuffieldfjo.org.uk)

- Ensure that contact plans are tailored to each child and regularly reviewed.

- Ensure skilled professional support is available.

A local authority is under a duty to allow a child '*reasonable contact*' with his parents *Children Act 1989 section 34(1)*) (and certain others) *Children Act 1989 section 34 (1)(b) – (d)*. This duty is supported by the general duty set out in *Schedule 2 para.15 Children Act 1989*, which applies "*unless it is not reasonably practicable or consistent with his welfare*".

A local authority, the child, or the parent may apply to the court for orders regulating contact. The court "*may make such order as it considers appropriate with respect to the contact which is to be allowed between the child and [that person]/ [any named person]*" *Children Act 1989 section 34(2), (3)*. The child's welfare is the court's paramount consideration[2]. The court must have regard to the welfare checklist[3], and must not make any order unless it would be better for the child than making no order at all[4].

A person who has made an application for an order under *section 34* which has been refused will be unable to make a further application with respect to the same child within 6 months of the date of refusal, without leave of the court[5]. This provision applies to both applications on granting an interim care order and on or after the granting of a full care order.

A local authority may make an application to the court for authorisation to "*to refuse to allow contact between the child and any person*" (one of those

---

2 Children Act 1989 section 1(1)

3 Children Act 1989 section 1(3)

4 Children Act 1989 section 1(5)

5 Children Act 1989 section 91(17)

identified by statute) and named in the order *Children Act 1989 section 34(4).*

When making a care order or interim care order the court may make a contact order even if no application has been made, if it takes the view that an order should be made[6].

In an urgent case, a local authority has the power to refuse to allow contact for up to seven days which would otherwise be required, if "*they are satisfied that it is necessary to do so in order to safeguard or promote the child's welfare*" *Children Act 1989 section 34(6).* For any longer period, the local authority would need to make a *section 34(4)* application to court.

Re T (Interim Care Order: Arrangements for contact) [2024] EWCA Civ 469 was an appeal by a local authority, supported by the children's guardian, from a case management order requiring them to arrange direct contact three times a week between the child and her mother. The Court of Appeal considered:

- The statutory framework for interim contact in care proceedings (in *schedule 2 para 15 Children Act 1989; Section 34 Children Act 1989*)

- The degree of welfare analysis required by the court when deciding on interim contact. The Children Act provides statutory framework and caselaw gives much useful guidance, but each case is highly fact specific.

- At an interim hearing, the relevant welfare factors are often not capable of being fully understood and are often nuanced and finely balanced. Judicial decision-making in relation to contact at

6 Children Act 1989 section 34(5)

every stage of the process case demands a careful and conscientious evaluation.

- That contact "*must not be allowed to destabilise or endanger the arrangements for the child*" (per Butler Sloss LJ, as she then was, in *Re B (Care: Contact: Local Authority's plans)* [1993] 1 FLR 543 at 551) retains its unimpeachable authority.

The Court of Appeal also consider the drafting and enforceability of recitals:

- Recitals in a children order shall appear at the end of the order.
- Recitals must only record necessary information, drafted in as short and neutral a manner as possible.
- Recitals should not record what happened in a hearing and should be limited to essential background matters which are not part of the body of the order.
- Any purported views of the court which did not form part of the court's decision should not be recited.
- Recording of a party's position before, during, or after a hearing as a recital should stop unless the template order requires such information to be recorded.

Post Adoption contact

On an adoption agency being authorised to place a child for adoption (or placing a child for adoption who is less than six weeks old) any child arrangements order[7] or order for contact with a child in care[8] will cease to have effect[9].

No application for contact can be made either for a child arrangements order or contact with a child in care whilst an adoption agency is authorised to place a child for adoption, or a child is placed for adoption[10]. However, court does have the power to make an order under *Adoption and Children Act 2002 section 26(2) (b)* on an application made by categories of people including parents[11]. The court can also make an order of its own initiative[12]. Before making a placement order the court is required to consider any contact proposed[13].

A placement order continues in force until it is either revoked by the court[14], or an adoption order is made or the child marries, forms a civil partnership or attains the age of 18 years[15]. A contact order made under *section 26* may cover a relatively short period between the making of a placement order and the subsequent granting of an adoption order, or, potentially longer periods if an early placement and adoption are not achieved. The power of the court to make an order under *section 26* is not confined to when the placement order is made, but extends to the entire period.

---

7 Children Act 1989 section 8

8 Children Act 1989 section 34

9 Adoption and Children Act 2002 section 26(1)

10 Adoption and Children Act 2002 section 26(2) (a)

11 Adoption and Children Act 2002 section 26 (3)

12 Adoption and Children Act 2002 section 26 (4)

13 Adoption and Children Act 2002 Section 27(4)

14 Adoption and Children Act 2004 section 24)

15 Adoption and Children Act 2002 section 21(4)

Orders for contact or for no contact can be made alongside an adoption order under the *Adoption and Children Act 2002*[16]. The court can also make an order of its own initiative when making an adoption order[17]. *Section 51A (3)(a) -(e) of the Adoption and Children Act 2002* identifies the categories of people who are permitted to be named in an order and includes any blood relatives or relatives through marriage or civil partnership.

Any person seeking an order for post-adoption contact must obtain the court's leave to pursue their application [18].In deciding whether leave should be granted, the court must consider *Adoption and Children Act 2002 section 51A (5)*:

- Any risk there might be of the application disrupting the child's life to such an extent they would be harmed by it.
- The applicant's connection to the child and
- Any representations by the child or the adoptive family.

A contact order made under *section 51A* may include directions as to how it is to be carried out or contain any conditions the court considers appropriate[19].

The factors for the court to consider when coming to a decision relating to the adoption of a child are set out in *Adoption and Children Act 2002 section 1 (4).* The paramount consideration must be the child's welfare, *throughout his life. Adoption and Children Act 2002 section 1 (2).*

---

16 Adoption and Children Act 2002 section 51A (2) (a) and (b)

17 Adoption and Children Act 2002 section 51A section (6)

18 Adoption and Children Act 2002 section 51A (4)(c)

19 Adoption and Children Act 2002 section 51B (1).

For many years, the default position has been indirect letter box contact only, for the child's minority.

Over the recent years there has been consideration of a "new approach," and a modernisation of post adoption contact. The President of the Family Division has spoken about how letter box contact can no longer be seen as the appropriate arrangement " *for most cases*" and the aim should be to maintain relationships with the people who were important to children before they were adopted speaking at the POTATO (Parents of Traumatised Adopted Teens Organisation) conference (17 May 2024); and at the '*Adapting Adoption to the Modern World*', Mayflower Lecture (Plymouth Law Society October 2023). The President highlighted the report of the Adoption sub-group of the Public Law Working Group.[20]

The President identified that there would need to be a change in culture. The target of the work was to establish the "default" position for future adopters so that the clear expectation will be that of maintaining birth family relationships as the starting point for every child, only to be ruled out where it is unsafe or unhelpful, as opposed to the current default with contact only being ruled in in exceptional circumstances.

The President's suggestions include:

- Contact should be seen as an integral part of the child's support package as they move on towards adoption, adolescence and adulthood. Contact should not be an 'add on' issue at placement order stage or at a final adoption hearing.

- The likely template for contact arrangements post adoption should be set at the placement order stage.

---

20 https://www.judiciary.uk/wp-content/uploads/2023/09/11-Sep-23-Report-v3.pdf

- It should be good practice for a *section 26 Adoption and Children Act 2002* contact order to contain a recital as to the court's view on contact arrangements post-adoption.

- Courts should look more widely in every case at with whom a child should maintain a relationship. This is particularly so when a child has siblings who are not likely to move with them to their adoptive home. There may be other relatives e.g. grandparents, uncles or aunts who may safely meet with a child, even where it is unsafe for parents to do so.

Recommendations from the Public Law Working Group include:

- The social worker should identify at the pre-proceedings stage people in the child's network who are significant to the child and who can play a role in post adoption contact. That role might include providing background information and ongoing news about significant family members, reassuring the child that they are remembered or facilitating a positive contact experience.

- The social worker's final statement should include an assessment of the ability of any identified person to maintain contact post adoption.

- The final statement should also include an analysis of all possible forms of contact, balancing the welfare benefits for the subject child against any safeguarding issues. If direct contact is not considered to be beneficial at this stage, it should recommend whether a reconsideration of direct contact should take place at a later stage.

- The adoption support plan should encompass a contact support plan, and this should be available in draft form for consideration by the court before making a placement order.

- An exploration of digital options for any letter box contact.

- Courts should consider, in the right case, making an order under *section 51A Adoption and Children Act 2002* to facilitate a review of contact by the court after the adoption order has been made.

In *Re B (A Child: Post-adoption contact)* [2019] EWCA Civ 29, in a discussion at the end of his judgment, the President of the Family Division stated "*The impact of new research and the debate is likely to be reflected in evidence adduced in court in particular cases. It may also surface in terms of advice and counselling to prospective adopters and birth families when considering what arrangements for contact may be the best in any particular case. But any development or change from previous practice and expectations as to post-adoption contact that may arise from these current initiatives will be a matter that may be reflected in welfare decisions that are made by adopters, or by a court, on a case by case basis. These are matters of 'welfare' and not of 'law'* ". The President stressed that the law in *Re R* [2005] EWCA Civ1128 continues to apply to applications for post-adoption contact and "*save for there being extremely unusual circumstances, no order will be made to compel adopters to accept contact arrangements with which they do not agree*".

In *Re A (A Child): Contested Adoption and Local Authority Conduct* [2024] EWFC 192 (B), a first instance decision by HHJ Roberts, a post-adoption contact order was made under *section 51A of the Adoption and Children Act 2002.*

The order provided for monthly staying contact between the father and child and a roadmap to work towards that staying contact starting. There was also consideration of a family assistance order to help with the development of contact.

The decision was fact specific. A was discharged from hospital following their birth to live with the foster carers. The parents were assessed as unable to safely parent A and care and placement orders were made.

The parents had another child, B, after the care and placement orders were made for A. The father (by then separated from the mother) was granted a child arrangements order for B. As the local authority had not placed A for adoption with the foster carers or found other adopters for her, questions arose whether it was necessary for A to be adopted at all.

Format of contact

The majority of post adoption contact with birth relatives is through letters being sent between birth and adoptive families via adoption agencies.

A more modern approach suggested is contact through digital platforms which could facilitate the 'letter' contact and also offer other less formal ways of staying in touch (photos, audio, video, emojis). Care does need to be taken with exchanging information that could show how a child looks or identifies the adopters or location of the adoptive placement, if there is a risk that the birth family might try to disrupt the placement. That has to be considered as part of the management of contact and is not a reason, in itself, to offer letter box contact only.

There are advantages and disadvantages to both digital and non-digital approaches. These highlight the need for:

- A tailored approach
- Relationship based
- Ease of accessibility
- Ability for plans to change and evolve including as children grow older and their needs evolve

There are however issues of concern that remain valid for both options.

Advantages of traditional 'letter box' contact include:

- Having a much-treasured letter to keep

Disadvantages of traditional letter box contact include:

- Letters are not informative
- They do not bring the other person to life
- Focused on the exchange of information rather than maintaining meaningful connections[21]

Advantages of digital contact include:

- For many children and young people communicating on digital platforms is something they are very comfortable with

Disadvantages of digital contact include:

- Digital poverty
- Low digital literacy skills
- Some people want an actual letter, a tangible object in their hands

Concerns around post adoption contact include:

- It is difficult for families to know if items are sent on, received and/or read.
- Lack of preparation

---

21 *Modernising post adoption contact: Findings from a recent consultation* https://www.nuffieldfjo.org.uk/wp-content/uploads/2021/08/nfjo_report_adoption_connections_20210913v2.pdf Nuffield Family Justice Observatory

- Lack of support for everyone involved
- Lack of support for birth parents with additional needs
- People do not know what to say, including fearing saying too much or the wrong thing
- Large gaps between communications
- Reading and writing difficulties
- Maintaining communication over time. PAC UK Big Consult[22] found that with participants in their study only 12% of letter box contact was still continuing after 6 or more years.
- Insufficient resources

With input from Adoption England, Family Rights Group has developed an interactive map to help birth families across England find adoption support and information in their area[23]. The resource is for birth relatives of children who have been adopted, are being adopted, or may be adopted, and who are looking for information or support. It includes advice and information about contributing to a child's life story work or life story book and support with contact with an adopted child, including letterbox contact

22 https://www.pac-uk.org/wp-content/uploads/2023/04/PAC-UK-Big-Consult-of-Adopted-People-FINAL.pdf

23 Support and information services for birth families affected by adoption in England – Family Rights Group (frg.org.uk)

Some specific examples

ARCBOX Communications APP is a digital life story platform. Children can contribute to a lasting digital record of their life. Unlike a traditional life story book, updates are instant and enable significant people within a child's life to contribute to their life story in real time. Children and their family can continue to contribute throughout their lives. All contributions must be approved by the life story editor (usually the child's social worker, other professional, or adopter) before the child can view them.

The ARCBOX messaging service allows communication using methods that are agreed in a communication plan e.g. note, letter, photo or card including by mobile App. Links can be created between people with whom the child has important relationships, including siblings living in separate placements. The life story editor will always see messages first, and approve them, before releasing them to the child's ARCBOX.

Charms

Charms is an App for digital life story work

Letter Swap

Is a digital letter box system that open to all regional adoption agencies.

Link Maker

All regional adoption agencies all have funding to use Link Maker.

Practice Points:

- Familiarise yourself with the case law in Public Law Working Group report, and the Public Law Working Group's interim report containing draft recommendations for best practice in respect of adoption (Appendix 1)

- Research in Practice's website has extensive information on managing post adoption contact[24]

- Be fully aware of any current research in this developing area, e.g. the on-going work of Professor Beth Neil (accessible through Research in Practice's website), including her team's research on the views of adopted adults on contact [25]

- Raise questions relating to post-adoption contact throughout the care and placement proceedings and adoption proceedings

- Ask the local authority to include post adoption contact in the final care plan setting out important relationships and the support that might be necessary to the child, the prospective adopters and birth family members

- Specific consideration of any sibling contact – what might not be safe if it involves adult birth family members might be safe for siblings

- Ask the local authority to address what independent support and counselling is available for birth parents

- Request the local authority actively to consider the full range of contact options and not rely on a generic letter box contact proposal

- Consider making an application for contact orders alongside placement orders under *Section 26 of the Adoption and Children Act 2002* so that the issue of post-adoption contact is identified

---

24 https://contact.rip.org.uk/

25 https://www.pac-uk.org/wp-content/uploads/2022/10/Maintaining-Relationships-with-Birth-Families-Research-Briefing.pdf

and discussed with potential adopters at an early stage in the process

- Consider the potential practical issues with face-to-face contact – duration, location, frequency, who should be present, expectations of the people involved, any risks

- Consider requesting a 'settling in' letter from the adoptive family to the birth family usually written a few months after the child has been placed and contains information about how the child has settled in with the family.

- Consideration should be given in every case to a meeting between the adopters and members of the birth family

CHAPTER EIGHT

CURRENT ISSUES

FDAC

Consideration of FDAC for cases involving substance misuse issue and the advantages of the FDAC process are considered in Chapter 4.

More frequently, FDAC is being utilised as a problem-solving court for other issues including domestic abuse. Recent research commissioned by the Nuffield Family Justice Observatory[1] included as one of their final recommendations whether and how some or all of the FDAC processes could be applied to parents with learning disabilities or difficulties to improve the effectiveness of support offered during and at the conclusion of care proceedings. FDAC's multi-agency approach, dynamic assessment, the extension to the court timetable to allow work to be undertaken and the possibility of post proceedings support during a supervision order would lend itself well to working with parents with a learning disability or difficulty.

London Borough A v A and others [2024] EWFC 46 was a case where the primary issues related to domestic abuse and neglect. In his judgment District Hughan said:

> "*It perhaps needs to be more widely recognised that the FDAC model can very successfully be used in cases where the main presenting difficulty is domestic abuse*". "*...it is also plain that the FDAC method of working is equally suitable to cases which involve domestic abuse and indeed mental health* ".

Babies in care proceedings : What do we know about parents with learning disabilities or difficulties June 2024

The local authority had identified this case as suitable for FDAC and had liaised with the clinical lead at FDAC who confirmed they were able to accommodate the case. On conclusion of proceedings the children were returned from foster care to the mother's care with a supervision order for 12 months.

The judge set out in a postscript the advantages of the proceedings being conducted in FDAC:

> "*I retain significant doubts that this outcome would have been achieved in standard care proceedings*".
>
> "*However, the FDAC model provides the support to help parents to achieve necessary changes. It is a dynamic and on-going assessment of a process. It isn't just a snapshot assessment. FDAC offers an assessment of how a parent responds to support and interventions.*"
>
> "*Without the consistent and intense nature of the support that the FDAC keyworker and team were able to put in place, I do not think we would have reached this outcome. Had the mother just been subject to assessment, absent of the keywork and other support, I fear that these children may have remained in foster care.*"

In domestic abuse cases there may be specific considerations e.g. separate non-lawyer reviews for each parent, the redaction of FDAC assessment reports, managing the sharing of progress reviews or non-lawyer review minutes.

Please see Chapter 4 for suggestions on how you might encourage a local authority to refer a case to FDAC.

Pause

The availability of support for parents on the conclusion of proceedings is not consistent. Support plans should be scrutinised in cases where children return/remain at home particularly when support started during proceedings and cases where parents have their own needs.

For parents whose children do not return/remain at home, the end of proceedings can mean the end of any interaction or support from professionals just when existing problems can be exacerbated (e.g. mental health, substance misuse) along with the grief, guilt, shame, stigma and isolation following the removal of a child.

Pause is a voluntary programme that works with women who have experienced or are at risk of experiencing repeat removals of children from their care. There are 19 Pause practices across 24 local authorities.[2]

Research shows that women in care proceedings continue to face a high risk of appearing in repeat sets of proceedings.[3]

- In England and Wales approximately 1 in 4 women are at risk of returning to court for subsequent care proceedings within 10 years of their first appearance in care proceedings

- The risk of returning to court is highest within the first 3 years after the initial proceedings. Following a first return to court, risk of further returns, increase

2 https://www.pause.org.uk/what-we-do/find-a-pause-practice/

3 *Mothers in recurrent care proceedings: new evidence for England and Wales* Nuffield Family Justice Observatory Alrouh et al. (2022) https://hubble-live-assets.s3.eu-west-1.amazonaws.com/birth-companions/file_asset/file/620/nfjo_eng_report_newborn_recurrence_20221111_final.pdf

- In both England and Wales, a high proportion of mothers in recurrent care proceedings (more than 40%) are estimated to be aged 14–19 at the birth of their first child

Pause works with women as individuals following the end of proceedings, offering intensive and tailored support to rebuild their lives rather than working with women to have their children returned to their care.

There is an 18-month programme of support, tailored to each individual woman's needs across a range of areas e.g. loss and grief, therapeutic needs, practical needs e.g. housing, activities, education and employment, based on the relationship between the woman and her Pause practitioner and with collaborations with partner agencies.

The criteria for women being accepted onto the programme are:

- Agreement to use a reversible contraceptive for the duration of the programme

- Being of childbearing age

- Not having children in their care and/ or not currently pregnant

You may want to discuss Pause with eligible clients before a final hearing to ensure support is in place immediately afterwards if there is a risk that a client might lose the care of her children and face returning home alone and isolated without support being available.

Other support for parents:

- Some local authorities have an inhouse model of support for parents who have had children removed

- Adult social care services

- Advocacy services

- Local voluntary sector organisations including peer support groups

- Adoption-related counselling services

The Family Rights Group has produced an interactive map for birth relatives of children who have been adopted, are being adopted, or may be adopted, and who are looking for information or support including advocacy support, counselling or therapeutic support.[4]

The Suspected Inflicted Head Injury Service (SIHIS) for children pilot

The Suspected Inflicted Head Injury Service for children is a pilot funded by the Department of Education (DfE) running until 31 March 2025. The trial is in three NHS trusts Manchester University Hospitals NHS Foundation Trust, Sheffield Children's NHS Foundation Trust and Birmingham Women and Children's NHS Foundation Trust. The service provides multi-disciplinary 'clinical hubs' running at each location, examining and reporting on cases of suspected inflicted head injuries in children under the age of eight referred in by the treating hospital. The hub will include access to paediatricians, paediatric radiology, ophthalmology, haematology, neurosurgery and neuroradiology, with availability from clinical genetics or orthopaedics to review cases.

The outcome of the SIHIS assessment is provided in a pro forma report. It brings together in one report the results of all the clinical investigations and will contain the SIHIS team's clinical assessment of the case. The report will be available to children's services, police, the courts and lawyers as the main record of the clinical evaluation. There are no specified timescales within which a report should be provided.

4 https://frg.org.uk/birth-families-map/

The pilot does not replace a parent's right to request a second opinion in the form of a rapid review from a critical care outreach team via the treating team – "Martha's Rule" being rolled out across the NHS from April 2024.[5]

SIHIS is a clinical trial rather than legal pilot. However, it does have a potential impact on any subsequently issued care proceedings.

Advantages (as stated by the pilot):

- Better and multidisciplinary diagnosis and treatment for children,
- Reduces the cost to the public purse of obtaining expert reports and the number of court appointed experts,
- Improving consistency and quality of reporting.

Concerns have been raised about the reports being used in care proceedings and the effect on the Article 6 and 8 rights of parents and children:

- Clinicians in the SIHIS pilot are professional witnesses of fact. Although it will be for the judge in care proceedings to decide on a case-by-case basis whether experts reports in proceedings will be "necessary", reports/investigations by the SIHIS hub pre proceedings will make it more difficult to meet the "necessity" test and justify the instruction of an independent expert in subsequently issued court proceedings.
- What role would parents have in choosing a hospital/expert from the pilot?

5 https://www.england.nhs.uk/patient-safety/marthas-rule/

- It is anticipated that questions for the SIHIS team will usually come from the local authority solicitor to the clinicians[6]. How will the parents' have any input into the instruction?

- Missing information that will not be available to the SIHIS e.g. pre proceedings there will not be the crucial statements of parents drafted within proceedings with the assistance of lawyers, or any other evidence that is acquired during the proceedings, e.g. access to full medical records, access to other evidence that might be before a court.

- Different experts having legitimately different views about these complex areas. How can judges and advocates identify areas of uncertainty without independent medical opinion report.[7]

- Complex medical evidence is not a safe area in which to trial producing a "uniform template."

- Under the *Family Procedure Rules 2010* an expert has a variety of duties to the court including Practice *Direction 25B 9.1* which deals with the contents of an experts report, which must:

  (f)

  (ii) describe the expert's own professional risk assessment process and process of differential diagnosis, highlighting factual assumptions, deductions from the factual

---

6 Paragraph 7 SIHIS-Questions-Answered-Sheet-August-2024.pdf (alc.org.uk).

https://www.lawgazette.co.uk/commentary-and-opinion/suspected-inflicted-head-injury-service-and-the-law-of-unintended-consequences/5120131.article

assumptions, and any unusual, contradictory or inconsistent features of the case;

(iii) indicate whether any proposition in the report is an hypothesis (in particular a controversial hypothesis), or an opinion deduced in accordance with peer-reviewed and tested technique, research and experience accepted as a consensus in the scientific community;

(iv) indicate whether the opinion is provisional (or qualified, as the case may be), stating the qualification and the reason for it, and identifying what further information is required to give an opinion without qualification;

(g) where there is a range of opinion on any question to be answered by the expert –

(i) summarise the range of opinion;

(ii) identify and explain, within the range of opinions, any 'unknown cause', whether arising from the facts of the case (for example, because there is too little information to form a scientific opinion) or from limited experience or lack of research, peer review or support in the relevant field of expertise;

(iii) give reasons for any opinion expressed: the use of a balance sheet approach to the factors that support or undermine an opinion can be of great assistance to the court;

What duties will the SIHIs clinicians have in relation to the contents of their reports?

The DfE has produced information for legal practitioners.

https://www.alc.org.uk/uploads/images/Legal-Practitioners-Awareness.pdf

Following the DfE SIHIS broadcast on 25 July 2024, a 'SIHIS Questions Answered document' has been provided from the DfE SIHIS-Questions-Answered-Sheet-August-2024.pdf (alc.org.uk).

Practice Points

- Request a copy the letter of instruction from the local authority.
- Request confirmation of the documents and information that have been considered by the SIHIS clinicians.
- Read the SIHIS proforma carefully. Does it refer to SIHIS multi-disciplinary meeting(s)? If so request the minutes or transcripts of the meetings.
- Request details of who attended any strategy meeting.
- The SIHIS report is a live document that will continue to be updated when further information is found or there is any additional testing. Check you have the most up to date document and the report is provided on a rolling basis if investigations are ongoing.
- Keep an eye out for evaluation reports on the trial published during the pilot.

CHAPTER NINE

TRANSPARENCY

The President of the Family Division's report *Confidence and Confidentiality: Transparency in the Family Courts*[1] sets out the competing needs for confidence and confidentiality in family proceedings including:

- Public interest
- Impact on public confidence of a closed system
- Learning and improvement for professionals involved in the family justice system
- Maintaining confidentiality around the identity and personal information of the children and adult parties whose cases become before the court
- Desire of many parties who come before the court not to have details of their private lives made public

Seminal research on reconciling the principle of transparency with the principle of respect for privacy (especially children's privacy) was carried out by Dr Julia Brophy et al.[2]

---

1 https://www.judiciary.uk/wp-content/uploads/2021/10/Confidence-and-Confidentiality-Transparency-in-the-Family-Courts-final.pdf)

2 https://corambaaf.org.uk/sites/default/files/PRD/Privacy%20and%20Safeguarding_Evaluation%20of%20Practice%20Guidance%202018_Children%20Judgments_May2021.pdf

This research recognises the far-reaching effects of information sharing through social media, and how that works in '*…a digital world with a perpetual footprint*', in the context of safeguarding and meeting the welfare needs of vulnerable children. It includes a study of judgments posted on BAILII between 2017 and 2020, and how readily children and their families could be identified even when not named, to help identify how better to anonymise judgments.

There are statutory restrictions on publishing information about proceedings concerning children.

> *Administration of Justice Act 1960 section 12*
>
> *Publication of information relating to proceedings in private.*
>
> *(1) The publication of information relating to proceedings before any court sitting in private shall not of itself be contempt of court except in the following cases, that is to say*
>
> *(a) where the proceeding*
>
> *(i) relate to the exercise of the inherent jurisdiction of the High Court with respect to minors;*
>
> *(ii) are brought under the Children Act 1989 or the Adoption and Children Act 2002; or*
>
> *(iii) otherwise relate wholly or mainly to the maintenance or upbringing of a minor;*
>
> *(2) Without prejudice to the foregoing subsection, the publication of the text or a summary of the whole or part of an order made by a court sitting in private shall not of itself be contempt of court except where the court (having power to do so) expressly prohibits the publication.*

(4) Nothing in this section shall be construed as implying that any publication is punishable as contempt of court which would not be so punishable apart from this section (and in particular where the publication is not so punishable by reason of being authorised by rules of court)

These restrictions apply after the conclusion of the proceedings.

Children Act 1989 section 97

Privacy for children involved in certain proceedings.

(2) No person shall publish to the public at large or any section of the public any material which is intended, or likely, to identify

(a) any child as being involved in any proceedings before the High Court or the family court in which any power under this Act or the Adoption and Children Act 2002 may be exercised by the court with respect to that or any other child; or

(b) an address or school as being that of a child involved in any such proceedings.

(4) The court or the Lord Chancellor may, if satisfied that the welfare of the child requires it and, in the case of the Lord Chancellor, if the Lord Chief Justice agrees, by order dispense with the requirements of subsection (2) to such extent as may be specified in the order.

(6) Any person who contravenes this section shall be guilty of an offence and liable, on summary conviction, to a fine not exceeding level 4 on the standard scale.

These restrictions apply during the proceedings.

Family Procedure Rules 2010 Rule 12.73 and *12.75* supplemented by *Practice Direction 12G* set out the groups of people to whom information relating to proceedings held in private (whether or not contained in a document filed with the court) may be communicated. This includes cases in which the "*where the court gives permission*" for information to be shared with particular people (*Family Procedure Rules Rule 12.73 (1*) (b))

Family Procedure Rules 2010 Rule 27.11 sets out the groups of people who are permitted to be present during a private hearing. These include:

- Duly accredited representatives of news gathering and reporting organisations (usually journalists and news reporters) *Family Procedure Rules 2010 Rule 27.11 (1) (f)*

- A duly authorised lawyer attending for journalistic, research or public legal educational purposes ('legal bloggers') *Family Procedure Rules 2010 Rule 27.11 (1) (ff)*

- Any other person with the court's permission *Family Procedure Rules 2010 Rule 27.11 (1) (g))*

The Transparency Implementation Group (TIG) was set up in 2021 to implement the planned changes to reporting on proceedings in the Family Court. It is judge led, and updates on TIG's work are published on the uk.gov judiciary website.[3]

As part of that work, the Family Court Transparency Pilot commenced in January 2023 and is now being piloted in 19 courts in relation to public law cases. The pilot permits is accredited journalists and 'legal bloggers' ("pilot reporters") to attend designated courts and report on what they see and hear ("the transparency principle"). All reporting is subject to the principles of the protection of children's privacy, through

---

3 https://www.judiciary.uk/about-the-judiciary/our-justice-system/jurisdictions/family-jurisdiction/transparency-implementation-group/

anonymity, unless the judge orders otherwise ("the anonymity principle"). The President of the Family Division issued *Transparency Reporting Pilot Guidance.* in January 2023 which was replaced in August 2024 with *The Reporting Pilot Guidance*[4]

The court may depart from the transparency principle in any case, and it retains a discretion to direct that there should be no reporting of the case. In deciding whether to restrict reporting, the Court must ensure the ECHR Article 6 rights of the parties to a fair trial are respected and must balance the Article 8 rights to respect for private and family life with and the Article 10 rights to freedom of expression[5].The court may also determine that there should be no reporting, or restricted or delayed reporting only of all, or part, of the proceedings. The court may also consider whether reporting should be restricted for a certain period or up to an event e.g. the conclusion of a criminal trial.[6]

The template transparency order is an important part of the Pilot. It is expressly stated on the face of the order that it is '*an injunction, which means that you must do what the order says.*'The template order also states, at paragraph 16, that:

1. Any documents provided to a reporter pursuant to this Order

> *a. Must not be shown or provided to any other person save as permitted by paragraph 15 above.*
>
> *b. Must be held securely and confidentially by the reporter.*
>
> *c. Must be kept for no longer than is necessary whereupon it must be securely destroyed or deleted.*

---

4 The Reporting Pilot Guidance (judiciary.uk)

5 *Re S (a child)* [2004] UKHL 47

6 The Reporting Pilot Guidance paragraphs ,23, 42 and 43

The template order provides that pilot reporters attending any hearing must be given a copy of the transparency order, so that they know the parameters within which they can operate. The order also provides that, on request, pilot reporters are entitled to be given copies of, or see, and quote from certain documents[7], i.e.:

- Documents drafted by advocates (or the parties, if they are litigants in person): case outlines, skeleton arguments, summaries, position statements, threshold documents, and chronologies

- Any indices from the court bundle

Any pilot reporter wishing to see any other document from the proceedings must apply to the court for permission.

The copy documents must be provided to the pilot reporter by digital transmission at a hearing that the pilot reporter is attending or within a reasonable time following the hearing. Pilot reporters should be prepared to offer a secure email address for digital transmission of documents by lawyers or lay parties. As it is not envisaged that documents will be redacted, any quotes from these documents must not breach the requirements for anonymity.

In *Tickle v Father & Ors* [2023] EWHC 2446 (Fam) Mrs Justice Lieven, in allowing an appeal to permit reporting of private law proceedings until final hearing, set out the following principles:

- Although Family Court proceedings are normally held in private the press and legal bloggers are entitled to attend under the Family Procedure Rules rule 27.11(2)(f).

7 The Reporting Pilot Guidance paragraph 49

- Such a person can be excluded, but only where it is "necessary" in the interests of the child, the safety or protection of parties or others, or the orderly conduct of proceedings *Family Procedure Rules rule 27.11(3).*

- In approaching the test of "necessity", what was said in *Re H-L (a child)*, albeit in a different legal context is a useful guide.

- It will rarely, but not never, be appropriate for the court to inquire as to why the journalist is seeking to report, or how s/he became aware of the hearing. If the judge becomes concerned that one party is seeking to use reporting as a litigation strategy, particularly in the context of issues around coercive control, the judge may wish to inquire into the background to the application to report. This can only be considered on a case specific basis.

- In determining whether a reporter can report on what they see and hear in the Family Court, the judge will have to apply a balance between Article 8 and Article 10 as in *Griffiths v Tickle* [2021] EWCA Civ 1882. The court will have to apply an "*intense focus*" on the "*comparative importance of the specific rights being claimed in the individual case...*"

- The child's best interest will be critical, although they will still have to be balanced against the other rights asserted. There may be an important distinction between cases, where the reporter is seeking to report wholly generic and systemic matters, and where the reporting is of the facts and evidence in the case, where the risk of identification of the child is much greater.

- There is a public interest in the reporting of cases in the Family Courts. There is a very real public interest in there being greater understanding of the work done by the Family Court.

- There may well be cases where it is appropriate to adjourn a decision about whether a case can be reported on until the final hearing. Whether that is justified must be considered on the facts of the individual case.

- In deciding whether to allow reporting, the views of the parties, including the child, are of great significance. However, they are not determinative, so no party holds a veto against reporting.

Re BR (Transparency Order: Finding of Fact Hearing) [2023] EWFC 9 was a public law case involving three different families in applications brought by three different local authorities (previously unconnected). Mr Justice Poole had previously determined that the fact-finding aspects of each case should be heard at a combined hearing, as each case related to allegations of fabricated or induced illness, and involved the children being treated at the same hospital. The hearing was due to start before the start of the pilot but for most of the hearing the pilot would be in effect. Poole, J decide to treat the case as if it was in the reporting pilot from the start of the hearing. He referred to the legal framework and leading case law. The judge made a transparency order adopting the template but varying it:

- Reporting was not permitted until criminal proceedings against all three mothers had been concluded and/or the police or Crown Prosecution Service have determined that criminal proceedings will not be brought, and no further action will be taken.

- Added a confidential schedule to the order in which the real names of the family members, including the children, because of the large number of parties in the case.

The judge also considered the concerns of the parties about jigsaw identification. He declined to make anything other than "*very limited additions to the information that may not be reported already listed in the template TO*" noting that pilot reporters are bound to take their responsibilities under s97 very seriously, *"and will naturally be cautious to avoid committing an offence"*. To assist reporters in avoiding jigsaw identification he added a schedule of seven pieces of information which could give rise to the jigsaw identification process.

At the Family Law Bar Association (FLBA) conference on 12 October 2024, The President of the Family Division confirmed the plan was for the reporting pilot to conclude as a pilot, and from 2025 the rules will be changed to allow the reporting of cases broadly in accordance with the approach used in the pilot.

Practice Points

- Know whether the court you are attending is or is not part of the Family Court Transparency Pilot.

- Be prepared if a reporter attends or wants to attend a hearing. The Transparency Project has produced updated guidance notes for pilot and non-pilot courts.

  https://transparencyproject.org.uk/wp-content/uploads/WHAT-TO-DO-WHEN-A-REPORTER-ATTENDS-RP-v-2-Jan-2024.pdf

  https://transparencyproject.org.uk/wp-content/uploads/WHAT-TO-DO-WHEN-A-REPORTER-ATTENDS-Non-RP-v-2-2024.pdf

- Ensure that you advise your client as fully as possible and take their instructions. It may help to focus on the possible effects (long as well as short term) of any publicity on the children in the case. HMCTS provides a helpful information sheet for parents and family members that can be shared with clients.[8]

- Familiarise yourself with the template transparency order[9] The court may modify the terms of the template order as appropriate depending on the facts of the case by the court's own motion, or by invitation.[10]

- Reassure your client of what cannot be reported e.g. names and addresses of child and parents, any information that could lead to jigsaw identification (e.g. names and/or locations of children's schools) and in cases involving alleged sexual abuse, the details of the alleged abuse.[11]

- Remind your client of the rules of confidentiality that bind them as well as everyone else.

- Update your standard letters to clients to include information about the pilot.

- Update your letters of instruction for experts to confirm that under the pilot that they can be named.[12]

---

8 https://www.judiciary.uk/wp-content/uploads/2023/06/TIG.Litigants.PlainEngGuide-v4-FIN.pdf

9 On the TIG website The TIG | Linktree

10 The Reporting Pilot Guidance paragraph 24

11 The Reporting Pilot Guidance paragraph 26

12 The Reporting Pilot Guidance paragraph 28 d) and f)

Published judgments

More transcripts of first instance decisions are being published by district and circuit judges on BAILII or the National Archives. There can be confusion about whether such judgments can be cited as authority for any particular argument. These judgments are examples of decisions made in particular cases. At most, they might be persuasive, but they do not create any binding legal precedent, unlike decisions of the Court of Appeal or the UK Supreme Court.

A published transcript of a judgment is not the same as a case reported in the formal law reports (e.g. the Family Law Reports or the Family Court Reports). These are selected for formal reporting e.g. because they create new principles or rules or clarify existing principles. A reported case is the most authoritative account of the court's decision, and transcripts of judgments should be used only if relevant but not reported.

Transparency in the Family Court Publication of Judgments Practice Guidance was issued by the President of the Family Division to provide practical advice to judges, legal advisers and magistrates to support publishing judgments.[13]

It is a guide to the process of anonymisation and how to avoid 'jigsaw identification' (drawing on the research of Dr Julia Brophy et al referred to above), together with a step-by-step account of the process of publication.

While there is no requirement for a case to fall within a certain category for it to be deemed suitable for publication, the making or refusal of a final care order or supervision order is listed a case type that might be

[13] Publication-of-Judgments-Practice-Guidance-JUNE-2024-1.docx (live.com)

suitable for publication. The following might be specifically considered for publication include[14]:

- The judgment involves a novel point of law or establishes a legal precedent; or
- The judge concludes that publication would be in the public interest for a fact specific reason; and
- A written judgment already exists in publishable form, or the judge has already ordered that the judgment be transcribed.

The guide sets out what the court should consider when deciding to publish a judgment, including the balancing exercise required as between ECHR Articles 6, 8 and 10 (and, where applicable, other rights).

Before deciding whether to publish a judgment, all parties should be notified so that they have an opportunity to make representations about publication and anonymisation. Advocates are expected to consider their instructions and their clients' interests, and raise any issues with the court when the question of publication becomes live.[15]

---

14 Transparency in the Family Court Publication of Judgments Practice Guidance 3.6

15 Transparency in the Family Court Publication of Judgments Practice Guidance 5.2

CHAPTER TEN

WORKING WITH CLIENTS

Practitioners such as family lawyer turned therapist Annmarie Carvalho and others have discussed the importance of family practitioners having a psychological understanding. Keeping in mind for example how our client's and our own attachment styles affect our interactions and learning to work with vulnerable clients in a psychologically informed way. That approach is important when working with clients in care proceedings who are often dealing with complex and unresolved trauma and are experiencing loss and grief.

Language and terminology

The Family Solutions Group have published a report *Language Matters*[1]. Aimed at separating families in private law proceedings, the core principles are applicable to public law proceedings:

- Plain English – avoid legal jargon and use words which can easily be understood rather than legal terminology
- Personal – use family names rather than legal labels. For example, using terms like the child, the mother, the father is dehumanising. Language should be focused on family members
- Proportionate – use language which is proportionate to the issues being considered.

1 https://www.familysolutionsgroup.co.uk/wp-content/uploads/2022/10/Language-Matters-October-2022-with-annexes.pdf

- Problem-solving – use constructive problem-solving language rather than battle language. For example, do not say the other side

- Positive futures – the emphasis is on building positive futures in which children can thrive.

We do need to be aware of the profound impact of choice of language when communicating with our clients about their cases. These choices can unintentionally perpetuate stigma and shame and some terminology is judgemental.

For example, the term 'substituted parenting', a term used by local authorities, usually negatively, when a parent needs such extensive support that the local authority regard it as detrimental to a child. Researchers found that parents were horrified by the term, as they felt powerless to avoid this 'substitution' or feeling being 'taken over' by professionals.[2]

TACT Fostering and Adoption *Language that Cares. Changing the way professionals talk about Children in Care*[3] is produced from research undertaken with children and young people about their wishes and feelings about the language used with or to talk about them. The report is a dictionary of words and phrases that professionals use with alternatives e.g. care plan = future plans, my plan; LAC review = my meeting, my review meeting, improving your time in care, [child's name]'s review.

---

2 Substituted Parenting: What does this mean for parents with learning disabilities in the family court context Nadine Tilbury and Beth Tarleton 2023 https://www.bristol.ac.uk/media-library/sites/sps/documents/wtpn/SP%20Report.pdf

3 https://www.tactcare.org.uk/content/uploads/2019/03/TACT-Language-that-cares-2019_online.pdf

Motivational Interviewing

As practitioners we are used to working in a way that uses linear thinking. Building cases for our clients, analysing, making rational arguments. Often taking what could be described as a parental or teacher role with clients.

Clients involved with children's services may feel shame, stigma and feel disempowered by the child protection process, fearful of the outcome and mistrustful of professionals[4]. Clients may be flooded with feelings and emotions.

Being too directive and assertive with emotionally heightened clients may make clients stop listening, become defensive, shut down, be reluctant to take on board advice/suggestions and/or do the opposite. Our response to that is often to keep repeating our message to our clients.

Motivational Interviewing is a therapeutic approach to communicating with clients. It is defined as:

> "*a person-centered, goal-oriented style of communication with particular focus on expressions of change. The goal is to increase personal motivation for and commitment to behavior change by eliciting and intensifying a person's own reasons for change in an atmosphere of acceptance and empathy*" *Motivational Interviewing*, William R Miller and Stephen Rollnick).

Working with, rather than against a client's feelings. If clients feel their voice is being heard and they have some degree of agency and autonomy, better outcomes may be achieved, and any changes are more likely to be sustained.

4 *Shame and guilt in child protection social work: new interpretations and opportunities for practice*, Matthew Gibson, 2013

Motivational Interviewing uses OARS:

- O – Open questions e.g. What support might help,
- A – Affirmation e.g. I can see how much you love and care for your child, it must be very difficult, it is a good thing to do to get help,
- R – Reflective listening e.g. You are feeling frustrated, and
- S – Summary reflections e.g. So I think you are saying x, is that right.

FDAC teams are trained in motivational interviewing, and it is considered to be one of the basic skills for FDAC teams and judges.[5]

For an introduction to Motivational Interviewing please see Annmarie Carvalho https://resolution.org.uk/the-review/archive/the-review-issue-221/motivational-interviewing-the-next-frontier-for-family-lawyers/. For further reading *Motivational Interviewing for working with children and families* (Forrester, Wilkins & Whittaker (2021)) aimed at social workers working in child protection and covering topics such as talking about serious concerns and consequences.

Trauma Informed approach

Trauma is when a person experiences very stressful, frightening or distressing events that are difficult to cope with or out of their control. It could be one incident, or an ongoing event that happens over a long period of time.[6]

---

5 https://fdac.org.uk/wp-content/uploads/2022/04/fdac-handbook-2021.pdf

6 https://www.mind.org.uk/information-support/types-of-mental-health-problems/trauma/about-

The 'window of tolerance' is a concept is when a person is coping well, thoughts are rational and emotions are calm. [7] It is a term commonly used to understand and describe brain/body reactions, especially following adversity. When a person is operating within this 'window', they can effectively manage and cope with their emotions, their nervous system is in a state of balance. Each individual's window of tolerance is different.

The accumulation of traumatic experiences, excessive stress or threats can affect a person's ability to stay within their 'window of tolerance' and activate the nervous system. Reactions can take over:

Hyper-arousal – commonly described 'fight or flight'. The sympathetic nervous system is overactivated. An inability to stay calm for example anxiety, anger, panic, racing thoughts, difficulty concentrating or

Hypo-arousal – commonly described as 'faint or freeze'. The parasympathetic nervous system is immobilized. The body wants to shut down, for example zone out, frozen, withdrawal, impact on long term memories being formed

Both can have physical and cognitive effects. NHS Lanarkshire's Ending Violence and Abuse (EVA) Services have produced a short animation (aimed at police officers) to give an understanding of the impact of trauma on the brain in survivors of abuse[8].The effect of trauma is not under conscious control.

---

trauma/#:~:text=Trauma%20is%20when%20we%20experience,that%20could%20be%20considered%20traumatic.

7 Introduced by Dan Siegel "The developing mind: Toward a neurobiology of interpersonal experience"

8 https://mediaco-op.net/projects/nhs-lanarkshires-eva-serviceanimation/

Adverse childhood experiences (ACEs) increase the likelihood of poor outcomes in adulthood in. The removal of a child is a traumatic event in itself, compounding any existing difficulties.[9] Trauma and adverse experiences impact on parenting. The impact of trauma and dealing with it could affect communication, the client's participation in proceedings and giving evidence. Parents might be triggered around the time of hearings, meetings, assessments and the legal process in general.[10]

How often do we read in documents that a parent is not engaging with professionals/the local authority? This label often travels with parents throughout the case. Why do parents resist or are reluctant to engage with professionals? "*There is growing realisation that the 'failure to engage' is more a question of services and professionals needing to do more to reach out and engage with people in trauma-informed ways*".[11]

Research shows[12] that 91.3% of solicitors/barristers in the sample said that they had not attended any formal training on trauma informed practice. 93% solicitors/barristers had not had any training on de-

---

9 *Child removal as the gateway to further adversity: Birth mother accounts of the immediate and enduring collateral consequences of child removal,* Broadhurst and Mason 2019 with accounts of the lived experience of child removal

10 *Recognising and minimising trauma in legal processes* Dr Laura Janes https://laurakjanes.co.uk/blog/recognising-and-minimising-trauma

11 *Parental Non-Engagement within Child Protection Services—How Can Understandings of Complex Trauma and Epistemic Trust Help?* Mason, Taggart, and Broadhurst 2020; *Reconceptualising parental non-engagement in child protection T*aggart, Mason, and Webb 2020)

12 "*People not just books: An Investigation into the Knowledge and Experience of Trauma Informed Practice in the Justice System"* Dr Catherine O'Neill https://www.intermediaries-for-justice.org/sites/default/files/dr_catherine_oneill_-_summary_of_research_.pdf https://www.intermediaries-for-justice.org/sites/default/files/compressed_people_not_just_books-_an_investigation_into_the_knowledge_and_understanding_of_trauma_informed_practice_in_the_justice_system_2-compressed_0.pdf

escalation techniques, recognising when people are 'overloading' and being equipped to manage this with the client.

A trauma informed approach:

- Acknowledges the impact of trauma on thoughts feelings and behaviour.
- Prevents further re-traumatisation.
- People need to feel safe to prevent further harm and re-traumatisation.
- Adopts a strengths-based approach.
- Builds trust.

Recognising and understanding the impact of trauma on our clients, and how adaptions can be made to support them is important. In terms of training, The Law Society of Scotland runs a trauma informed lawyer certification course[13].

Practice points

- Minimise the time the client spends re living incidents of trauma.
- Explain why we are asking sensitive questions.
- Acknowledge the client's experience.

13 https://www.lawscot.org.uk/members/cpd-training/events/trauma-informed-lawyer-certification-course/

- Allow the client control over when and how they talk about their traumatic experiences.

- Ask what has the client found helpful in the past.

- Consider including the impact of trauma in the 1-page profile that you prepare with your client (See Chapter 4)

- Establish and maintain boundaries with clients.

Self-care and managing trauma

Representing parents in care proceedings is a privilege, often acting for the most disadvantaged in society, vulnerable and traumatised clients, at the most difficult moments in their lives.

We are routinely exposed to high levels of vicarious trauma and stress in our day-to-day case work. We balance court deadlines, targets, working at legal aid rates and an "always on culture".

There has been an increase in awareness and interest in stress, burn out and well-being in the legal profession in recent years (e.g. as described by the President of the Family Division in 2019[14] and Resolution's well-being survey[15]). Vicarious trauma is a live issue for care practitioners, for which most practitioners have received no formal education or training.

---

14 https://www.wellbeingatthebar.org.uk/2019/06/19/wellbeing-and-the-family-justice-system-by-sir-andrew-mcfarlane-president-of-the-family-division/

15 https://resolution.org.uk/wp-content/uploads/2021/05/Resolution-Wellbeing-Report-FINAL.pdf

Vicarious trauma i.e. not experiencing trauma directly but being exposed to it, is an inevitability for those representing parents in care cases. It can be caused by:

- Listening to clients, reading witness statements/medical reports, listening to 999 recordings, viewing body worn camera footage etc.

- Being with clients in crisis.

Although individuals will respond in different ways, continuing exposure to trauma through our case work does lead to negative effects.

Our own well-being is vital. Workplace support is crucial including supervisor support, peer support and trauma training. For more information including individual, peer, team, organisational and profession wide action see *Vicarious Trauma in the Legal Profession: A practical guide to trauma, burnout and collective care* by Joanna Fleck and Rachel Francis. Also "*The case that really got to me: An introduction to family law supervision*" by Christopher Mills for family law supervision and reflective practice.

LawCare offers free confidential support, information and training to the legal sector to help with mental health and wellbeing problems https://www.lawcare.org.uk/ .

MORE BOOKS BY LAW BRIEF PUBLISHING

A selection of our other titles available now:-

'A Practical Guide to the Independent School Standards – September 2023 Edition' by Sarah McKimm
'A Practical Guide to Estate Administration and Crypto Assets' by Richard Marshall
'A Practical Guide to Managing GDPR Data Subject Access Requests – Second Edition' by Patrick O'Kane
'A Practical Guide to Parental Alienation in Private and Public Law Children Cases' by Sam King QC & Frankie Shama
'Contested Heritage – Removing Art from Land and Historic Buildings' by Richard Harwood QC, Catherine Dobson, David Sawtell
'The Limits of Separate Legal Personality: When Those Running a Company Can Be Held Personally Liable for Losses Caused to Third Parties Outside of the Company' by Dr Mike Wilkinson
'A Practical Guide to Transgender Law' by Robin Moira White & Nicola Newbegin
'A Practical Guide to 'Stranded Spouses' in Family Law' by Mani Singh Basi
'A Practical Guide to Residential Freehold Conveyancing' by Lorraine Richardson
'A Practical Guide to Pensions on Divorce for Lawyers' by Bryan Scant
'A Practical Guide to Challenging Sham Marriage Allegations in Immigration Law' by Priya Solanki
'A Practical Guide to Digital Communications Evidence in Criminal Law' by Sam Willis
'A Practical Guide to Legal Rights in Scotland' by Sarah-Jane Macdonald
'A Practical Guide to New Build Conveyancing' by Paul Sams & Rebecca East
'A Practical Guide to Defending Barristers in Disciplinary Cases' by Marc Beaumont
'A Practical Guide to Inherited Wealth on Divorce' by Hayley Trim
'A Practical Guide to Practice Direction 12J and Domestic Abuse in Private Law Children Proceedings' by Rebecca Cross & Malvika Jaganmohan

'A Practical Guide to Confiscation and Restraint' by Narita Bahra QC, John Carl Townsend, David Winch
'A Practical Guide to the Law of Forests in Scotland' by Philip Buchan
'A Practical Guide to Health and Medical Cases in Immigration Law' by Rebecca Chapman & Miranda Butler
'A Practical Guide to Bad Character Evidence for Criminal Practitioners by Aparna Rao
'A Practical Guide to Extradition Law post-Brexit' by Myles Grandison et al
'A Practical Guide to Hoarding and Mental Health for Housing Lawyers' by Rachel Coyle
'A Practical Guide to Psychiatric Claims in Personal Injury – 2nd Edition' by Liam Ryan
'Stephens on Contractual Indemnities' by Richard Stephens
'A Practical Guide to the EU Succession Regulation' by Richard Frimston
'A Practical Guide to Solicitor and Client Costs – 2nd Edition' by Robin Dunne
'Constructive Dismissal – Practice Pointers and Principles' by Benjimin Burgher
'A Practical Guide to Religion and Belief Discrimination Claims in the Workplace' by Kashif Ali
'A Practical Guide to the Law of Medical Treatment Decisions' by Ben Troke
'Fundamental Dishonesty and QOCS in Personal Injury Proceedings: Law and Practice' by Jake Rowley
'A Practical Guide to the Law in Relation to School Exclusions' by Charlotte Hadfield & Alice de Coverley
'A Practical Guide to Divorce for the Silver Separators' by Karin Walker
'The Right to be Forgotten – The Law and Practical Issues' by Melissa Stock
'A Practical Guide to Planning Law and Rights of Way in National Parks, the Broads and AONBs' by James Maurici QC, James Neill et al
'A Practical Guide to Election Law' by Tom Tabori
'A Practical Guide to the Law in Relation to Surrogacy' by Andrew Powell
'A Practical Guide to Claims Arising from Fatal Accidents – 2nd Edition' by James Patience
'A Practical Guide to the Ownership of Employee Inventions – From Entitlement to Compensation' by James Tumbridge & Ashley Roughton
'A Practical Guide to Asbestos Claims' by Jonathan Owen & Gareth McAloon

'A Practical Guide to Stamp Duty Land Tax in England and Northern Ireland' by Suzanne O'Hara
'A Practical Guide to the Law of Farming Partnerships' by Philip Whitcomb
'Covid-19, Homeworking and the Law – The Essential Guide to Employment and GDPR Issues' by Forbes Solicitors
'Covid-19 and Criminal Law – The Essential Guide' by Ramya Nagesh
'Covid-19 and Family Law in England and Wales – The Essential Guide' by Safda Mahmood
'A Practical Guide to the Law of Unlawful Eviction and Harassment – 2nd Edition' by Stephanie Lovegrove
'Covid-19, Brexit and the Law of Commercial Leases – The Essential Guide' by Mark Shelton
'A Practical Guide to Costs in Personal Injury Claims – 2nd Edition' by Matthew Hoe
'A Practical Guide to the General Data Protection Regulation (GDPR) – 2nd Edition' by Keith Markham
'Ellis on Credit Hire – Sixth Edition' by Aidan Ellis & Tim Kevan
'A Practical Guide to Working with Litigants in Person and McKenzie Friends in Family Cases' by Stuart Barlow
'Protecting Unregistered Brands: A Practical Guide to the Law of Passing Off' by Lorna Brazell
'A Practical Guide to Secondary Liability and Joint Enterprise Post-Jogee' by Joanne Cecil & James Mehigan
'A Practical Guide to the Pre-Action RTA Claims Protocol for Personal Injury Lawyers' by Antonia Ford
'A Practical Guide to Neighbour Disputes and the Law' by Alexander Walsh
'A Practical Guide to Forfeiture of Leases' by Mark Shelton
'A Practical Guide to Coercive Control for Legal Practitioners and Victims' by Rachel Horman
'A Practical Guide to the Law of Driverless Cars – Second Edition' by Alex Glassbrook, Emma Northey & Scarlett Milligan
'A Practical Guide to TOLATA Claims' by Greg Williams
'A Practical Guide to Elderly Law – 2nd Edition' by Justin Patten
'A Practical Guide to Responding to Housing Disrepair and Unfitness Claims' by Iain Wightwick

'A Practical Guide to the Law of Bullying and Harassment in the Workplace' by Philip Hyland
'How to Be a Freelance Solicitor: A Practical Guide to the SRA-Regulated Freelance Solicitor Model' by Paul Bennett
'A Practical Guide to Prison Injury Claims' by Malcolm Johnson
'A Practical Guide to the Small Claims Track – 2nd Edition' by Dominic Bright
'A Practical Guide to Advising Clients at the Police Station' by Colin Stephen McKeown-Beaumont
'A Practical Guide to Antisocial Behaviour Injunctions' by Iain Wightwick
'Practical Mediation: A Guide for Mediators, Advocates, Advisers, Lawyers, and Students in Civil, Commercial, Business, Property, Workplace, and Employment Cases' by Jonathan Dingle with John Sephton
'The Mini-Pupillage Workbook' by David Boyle
'A Practical Guide to Crofting Law' by Brian Inkster
'A Practical Guide to the Law of Domain Names and Cybersquatting' by Andrew Clemson
'A Practical Guide to the Law of Gender Pay Gap Reporting' by Harini Iyengar
'NHS Whistleblowing and the Law' by Joseph England
'Employment Law and the Gig Economy' by Nigel Mackay & Annie Powell
'A Practical Guide to Noise Induced Hearing Loss (NIHL) Claims' by Andrew Mckie, Ian Skeate, Gareth McAloon
'An Introduction to Beauty Negligence Claims – A Practical Guide for the Personal Injury Practitioner' by Greg Almond
'Intercompany Agreements for Transfer Pricing Compliance' by Paul Sutton
'Zen and the Art of Mediation' by Martin Plowman
'A Practical Guide to the SRA Principles, Individual and Law Firm Codes of Conduct 2019 – What Every Law Firm Needs to Know' by Paul Bennett
'A Practical Guide to Adoption for Family Lawyers' by Graham Pegg
'A Practical Guide to Industrial Disease Claims' by Andrew Mckie & Ian Skeate
'A Practical Guide to Conducting a Sheriff Court Proof' by Andrew Stevenson
'A Practical Guide to Vicarious Liability' by Mariel Irvine
'A Practical Guide to Applications for Landlord's Consent and Variation of Leases' by Mark Shelton
'A Practical Guide to Relief from Sanctions Post-Mitchell and Denton' by Peter Causton

'A Practical Guide to Equity Release for Advisors' by Paul Sams
'A Practical Guide to Financial Services Claims' by Chris Hegarty
'The Law of Houses in Multiple Occupation: A Practical Guide to HMO Proceedings' by Julian Hunt
'Occupiers, Highways and Defective Premises Claims: A Practical Guide Post-Jackson – 2nd Edition' by Andrew Mckie
'A Practical Guide to Financial Ombudsman Service Claims' by Adam Temple & Robert Scrivenor
'A Practical Guide to Running Housing Disrepair and Cavity Wall Claims: 2nd Edition' by Andrew Mckie & Ian Skeate
'A Practical Guide to Holiday Sickness Claims – 2nd Edition' by Andrew Mckie & Ian Skeate
'Arguments and Tactics for Personal Injury and Clinical Negligence Claims' by Dorian Williams
'A Practical Guide to Drone Law' by Rufus Ballaster, Andrew Firman, Eleanor Clot
'A Practical Guide to Compliance for Personal Injury Firms Working With Claims Management Companies' by Paul Bennett
'RTA Allegations of Fraud in a Post-Jackson Era: The Handbook – 2nd Edition' by Andrew Mckie
'RTA Personal Injury Claims: A Practical Guide Post-Jackson' by Andrew Mckie
'On Experts: CPR35 for Lawyers and Experts' by David Boyle
'An Introduction to Personal Injury Law' by David Boyle

These books and more are available to order online direct from the publisher at www.lawbriefpublishing.com, where you can also read free sample chapters. For any queries, contact us on 0844 587 2383 or mail@lawbriefpublishing.com.

Our books are also usually in stock at www.amazon.co.uk with free next day delivery for Prime members, and at good legal bookshops such as Wildy & Sons.

We are regularly launching new books in our series of practical day-to-day practitioners' guides. Visit our website and join our free newsletter to be kept informed and to receive special offers, free chapters, etc.

You can also follow us on Twitter at www.twitter.com/lawbriefpub.

www.ingramcontent.com/pod-product-compliance
Lightning Source LLC
LaVergne TN
LVHW052316200926
848481LV00002B/580
* 9 7 8 1 9 1 6 6 9 8 3 1 4 *